REVENUE
ROCKET

REVENUE ROCKET

"Revenue Rocket is essential reading for anyone who hopes to succeed with channel partners. I love the chapter 'Ten Mistakes to Avoid with Partners.'"

Robert C. DeMarzo
V.P. Editorial Director, VARBusiness Magazine

"The Technology Adoption Life Cycle is famous for wreaking havoc on partner and channel relationships. John Addison knows the ins and outs of this problem very well and his analysis and recommendations are a must read for any marketing executive in the high tech sector."

Geoffrey Moore
Author, *Crossing the Chasm, Inside the Tornado, Living on the Fault Line*

"Revenue Rocket shows that distribution channels are the critical core to 21st-century sales and marketing strategy. This compelling book shows how to establish and develop loyal channel partners. By making them successful, you'll experience your own Revenue Rocket."

Joe Womack, Vice President
Sun Microsystems

"Revenue Rocket gives energy companies the commercialization and marketing strategies necessary to succeed in the hydrogen economy."

Henry Wedaa
President, California Hydrogen Business Council

"A great roadmap for success. John Addison shows us how to get the best sales partners and make them successful. Your competition won't know what hit them."

Guy Kawasaki,
Author, *Rules for Revolutionaries, Selling the Dream*

"John Addison, as our consultant, helped us consistently outperform. Now his powerful consulting strategies are in this book. The big idea in each chapter gives you the game plan. The action plans show you how to get results."

Bob Eubank, President
American Legacy Products

"DIrect, concentrated, action oriented. Every executive should read Revenue Rocket to understand how to involve channel partners in making your product a success."

Vipin Kumar, CEO
VIPRI

"Revenue Rocket is essential reading if you want to succeed with channel partners, solution integrators, and strategic alliances."

Mendel Stafford, Manager, EDS

"Revenue Rocket is a book that every high-tech marketing and channel executive should read. John Addison makes it easy to read and understand the real-world strategies that create market leadership and channel partner loyalty."

Philippe Lavie, President
KeyRoad Enterprises

"Everyone who sells and markets through international distributors should read this book. Revenue Rocket explains how to secure the best channel partners, become their most important supplier, and motivate them to proactively sell your products."

Elizabeth Budzynska, Vice President of Global Sales
and Business Development, Aethra

"Revenue Rocket delivers powerful strategies that will challenge you to re-assess your company's approach to market leadership, strategic alliances, and sustained channel partner success."

Robert De Martino, Vice President
Sun Microsystems

REVENUE ROCKET

New Strategies for Selling With Partners

John Addison

Revenue Rocket:
New Strategies for Selling with Partners

Published by ProStar *Publications*, Inc.

FIRST EDITION

ISBN 157785-389-X

Library of Congress Control 2002110506

Addison, John
Revenue Rocket: New strategies for selling with partners /John Addison – First Edition
1. Sales. 2. Marketing. 3. Distribution Channels. 4.Industrial Management. I. Title

Contents

PART THREE
SALES LEVERAGE

About the Author

John Addison is president of OPTIMARK, a leading consulting firm focused on sales channel strategy and partner development. OPTIMARK, based in Silicon Valley, has helped technology leaders grow their businesses. These leaders include Sun Microsystems, General Electric, Veritas, and QLogic.

Mr. Addison is also on the advisory boards of breakthrough, early-stage companies. Mr. Addison provides early-stage consulting to companies who achieved successful IPOs.

His workshops and speeches are popular in the Americas, Europe, and Asia, including conferences of sales professionals and solution integrators.

Prior to founding OPTIMARK, Mr. Addison was an area channel manager for Sun Microsystems. For three years, he led a sales team to 300% annual growth in 15 states, from $4 million to $110 million. Mr. Addison is considered one of the early architects of Sun's highly successful channel programs. You can reach John Addison at john@optimarkworks.com.

How to Read this Book

In One Minute

Flip through the pages. Assume that there is nothing new. Then watch your friends sell circles around you.

In One Hour

You can get some good results in one hour. Read the big ideas in each chapter. Think about how they apply to your business. Look at the visual models. Take action.

In One Day

You can read this book in one day. You will be armed with new ideas and models to permanently improve your sales. You will even have time to think about how you will apply the ideas to your business.

In One Week

You can dramatically improve your sales by reading a couple of chapters per day. You will have time to seriously think about the implications of these new sales and partner channel strategies. You can write some good action items.

In One Month

In one month you can change the world. Take a chapter every other day. Think. Discard obsolete approaches. Build personal goals and action items based on the recommended action at the end of each chapter. Implement new strategies that give you a permanent competitive advantage. Build a Revenue Rocket.

Introduction

You will increase revenue with the strategies in this book: Discover new ways to inspire your sales partners to achieve record sales for you; uncover fresh approaches from the real-life success stories in this book; and accelerate sales every time you launch a new product or service.

Competition is real-time and is intense. Customers are permanently won, or lost, based on sales partners who either recommend your products or those of your competition. Your success or failure is determined by how others sell, market, integrate, and support what you offer.

This book is geared toward those executives, marketing managers, and sales professionals who involve partners to better sell and to better support their customers. Its intended goal is to give you the strategies and details of effectively working with different types of partners, including solution providers, resellers, and strategic partners. You will see how great companies treat these organizations, and their people, as partners rather than resellers.

Solution providers make products part of complete customer solutions. In different industries they go by various names such as system integrators, service providers, original equipment manufacturers (OEMs), and value-added resellers. For example, Hewlett- Packard is an important OEM partner of Intel. Accenture is a solution integrator partner for Microsoft.

Resellers sell products for a variety of firms. Resellers compete on price and customer convenience. In different industries they go by names such as retailers, eCommerce sites, rep firms, and distributors. Wal-Mart is an important reseller for Sara Lee and Campbell Soup.

Alliance partners complement products and make them more important to customers. They often do not resell the products. Oracle software makes Sun Microsystems computers more valuable to many customers, and vice-versa. They are alliance partners.

Collectively these partners are often viewed as channels of distribution. Large companies have complex channels of distribution including distributors between the company and specialized partners. These selling partners are often referred to as a channel partners.

Launch a Revenue Rocket with the best practices in managing distribution channels, direct sales, and strategic partners. Involve the best partners at the right time with the ideal strategy. This book details how to implement the best channel strategies. The book includes 110 action items, and 10 things to avoid while increasing channel sales. The book progresses through these three sections:

✓ **Market Leadership**
✓ **Partner Excellence**
✓ **Sales Leverage**

Market leadership results from providing the best solutions for groups of customers. Customers vote for leaders with each buying decision. Case studies will show how some corporations are best at cost leadership, customer intimacy, or creative products. New product launches often are decisive in creating new leaders and undermining the competitive power of the old. The market leadership section of this book, also details the strategy of achieving leadership in one customer community at a time. Channel strategy starts with market leadership strategy.

Partner Excellence, the second section of this book, goes to the heart of how to achieve lasting sales growth with new strategies for selling with partners. Unveiled are guidelines about ideal channel partner coverage, winning partner loyalty, empowering partners to executive your marketing campaigns, and compelling distribution channel partners to make you number one.

Sales Leverage, the final section of this book, shows how to accelerate revenue by focusing direct sales and channel sales on appropriate customers and markets. Understand why having both direct sales and channel partners are important. You will see how to improve partner relationships and reduce conflict.

There has never been a greater need for better strategy, because the sales profession has reached a new level of complexity. Customers want complete solutions. They want to order 24 hours per day. Companies use sophisticated combinations of sales and channel partners to meet these customer needs. *Revenue Rocket* shows how it all fits together.

For this author, working with technology leaders has been invaluable. I have helped major firms like Sun Microsystems, and one-time startups like Internet Security Systems, succeed with the right channel strategies and their implementation. In high technology, you rapidly learn what works, what does not work, and how to quickly adapt.

Powerful lessons have been learned working with channel partners in Europe, Asia, and the Americas. Nowhere are the lessons more intense than here in Silicon Valley. Venture capitalists bet billions. Some companies explode into superstars like Cisco, Sun Microsystems, Oracle, Genentech, and Charles Schwab. Others have their day, and then disappear.

This book organizes these lessons into powerful strategies. It shows you how to implement and succeed. Each chapter concludes with action items that can help you succeed quickly. You are warned about the pitfalls and how to avoid them. You will explore strategies to build market leadership, launch new products, develop the right channel partners, and to improve your sales priorities. You will look at companies who succeed and some who fail.

The ultimate winners provide customers with better solutions. The leaders achieve competitive advantage by implementing these new strategies for selling with partners.

Enjoy your new leadership and success,

John Addison

www.optimarkworks.com

Part One

Market Leadership

1

First to Market

Be first to market with a new product. This gives you a permanent competitive advantage. Achieve leadership in one customer community at a time. Use the right partners, at the right time.

New Strategies for Selling with Partners

Launch a Revenue Rocket with the strategies in this book. Inspire your partners to achieve record sales. Accelerate channel growth with each new product launch. Improve partner relationships and reduce conflict.

We are in a period of transition. The old strategies centered on resellers, not selling partners. Strategies focused on fulfillment, stuffing channels, and bypassing resellers once sales started doing well. The new strategies for selling with partners center on market leadership, partner excellence, and sales leverage.

Help your corporation discard the old strategies like "one size fits all" distribution channels, motivating resellers only with price, and generic promotions. Achieve sustained growth with new strategies including meeting the lifetime needs of customer communities, selectively partnering with the best, helping partners achieve excellence, empowering different partners at different stages of the product lifecycle, and working with partners instead of around them.

Anytime, Anywhere

This is our first lesson in market leadership. One billion people have changed the way that they work, play, compute, and communicate thanks to Bill Joy and his team. Bill Joy is a brilliant computer scientist and a founder of Sun Microsystems. To think big, Bill Joy started by thinking small. While many scientists focused on impossibly complex supercomputers, Bill Joy focused on the power of millions of small computers and devices working together.

Bill envisioned information and computer applications being available to all. At the time of his vision, information was stuck in "boxes" like PCs, servers, mainframes, and workstations. He wanted the information to be easily accessed across networks. He wanted to free the Internet from only being available to a few researchers. Beyond just information, he envisioned harnessing the collective power of all the computers on the network. Millions embraced this vision – "The network is the computer."

Sun Labs was created to give exceptional talent, like Bill Joy, an environment where they could create the future of network computing. Many of these bright engineers were located in Aspen, Colorado, to shelter them from corporate bureaucracy. After being threatened with a lawsuit from a Los Angeles tanning salon, the group was forced to drop the name Sun Labs. Their new slogan was "Sun Microsystems Laboratories – not your average tanning salon."

In another setback, a key software developer named Patrick Naughton announced he was leaving Sun. Patrick's manager asked him for an email documenting what should be changed at Sun. Patrick documented the frustration of Sun's software engineers with an unworkable amalgamation of programming interfaces. Scott McNealy agreed with the assessment. Soon Patrick Naughton, Bill Joy, James Gosling, and an elite secret team were focused on creating a single operating environment and a single programming language.

In 1991, James Gosling, made the vision of one language a reality. The language was ultimately named "Java," either because of brand marketing brilliance, or because the computer scientists were loaded with too much caffeine. Java was a new computer language that could run on virtually all computers from giant mainframes to small palm devices. Growing teams of engineers enhanced Java.

Bill and James recognized that most innovation had to come from outside Sun. The task of one environment for millions of smart electronics was too much for Sun alone. Java need to run effectively on IBM mainframes, Microsoft operating systems, Nokia cell phones, Palm computers, Sony televisions, and so on. Sun wanted to be a platform for millions of engineers and software developers.

Non-conventional thinking was again required. A rule of marketing is to give away razors so that a fortune can be made selling razor blades. Sun reversed that thinking and gave away millions of copies of Java "razor blades", so that Sun could be at the center of the computing universe "razor." Specifically, Sun could be at the center of a non-Microsoft universe. Of special importance were the programmers who would create applications that gave Java value. Needed were revolutionaries.

Fire-Breathing Revolutionaries

The first 90 percent of a revolution is creating the product or service; the second 90 percent is evangelizing it. At the beginning of a revolution, you need evangelists, not sales, because leverage spreads news. . . .Evangelism is the process of getting people not just to buy, but also to believe in your product, service, or company so much that they are compelled to make converts for you.

Guy Kawasaki
Rules for Revolutionaries

The revolution was on. Programmers embraced the idea of Java allowing them to write a program only once, instead of tediously rewriting it for different computers and operating systems. They embraced Java for being object oriented, so that code could be reused. They embraced the idea that many small programs networked together were better than a massive "bug-filled" program. A small Java program was embraced as beautiful. A large program, in Bill Joy's words, "is like having an elephant living in your apartment."

Breakthroughs do not find an easy path to commercial success. The vision of Java flew in the face of companies and partners making a good living from proprietary approaches. Microsoft and Intel profited from having applications only running on Windows on PCs with Intel inside. IBM profited from having applications only run on IBM mainframes and AS400s. Nokia was a cell phone market leader by offering unique applications for its phones. If Java were to succeed, it would need to be in one application at a time. Capturing the entire market immediately was not an option.

Netscape came to the rescue when it decided to include Java in every Netscape Internet browser. With Java in Netscape small applications could be delivered with information. With this approach, the Internet seemed much faster for applications where less information needed to be sent to smart browsers at the other end of the network. For example, online customers of stockbrokers could have their account information updated much faster.

Visionaries and Competitive Advantage

Tens of millions started using the Netscape Browser with its built-in ability to run small Java applications. Visionaries started to dream of gaining competitive advantage. Scottish Telecom saw a way to provide better network services faster than its rival British Telecom. Soon British Telecom competed by doing more software projects in Java. Reuters saw a greatly expanded market in every browser running Java. The brokerage firm of Dean Witter offered customers a new generation of online services, while staid brokerage firms on Wall Street warned customers to avoid the Internet altogether. Home Depot saw the advantages of writing applications once from smart Internet browsers, smart cash registers, and smart devices for all employees.

Major software companies jumped on the bandwagon. Java gave them a better architecture. It promised to save millions by avoiding the massive cost of rewriting their applications to many environments. Announcements of planned Java applications came from Oracle, SAP, Siebel, Reuters,

21

TIBCO, and PeopleSoft. Early demos started appearing for applications in manufacturing, finance, customer relationship management, telecommunications, education, and more.

If one believed everything in the press releases, PowerPoint presentations, and magazine articles, Java had already changed the world. As a consultant, Sun asked me to create a two-day workshop for its channel partners that espoused Java. I traveled the country touting Java to these partners. I saw the enthusiasm, I heard of the early customer successes, and I heard about the problems. Faster performance was demanded. More tools were desired. More enterprise software was deemed necessary.

In fact, innovation never creates a full-blown, instant, commercial success. The railroad took years, as did radio, and television. Imagine complaints about buying an early telephone. Who would be the first to complain when there was no one else to call and no telephone network?

Java performance, however, did improve. A Java Virtual Machine became widely available on my platforms. The promise of running Java on more computers than any other platform became a reality. This Java evangelism was embraced in my workshops. Java partnerships grew. Applications grew. Soon, one hundred million people were running Java in the Internet browser.

Oracle, the world's leading database software firm, delivered on its promise to incorporate Java in its leading software products. Oracle competitors Microsoft and IBM started to worry about missing out on something big.

IBM showed rare agility for an established leader that had much to lose from the Java revolution. IBM could have taken the approach of trying to keep customer applications "locked in" to IBM's closed mainframe and minicomputer architecture. Java could hurt IBM hardware sales. IBM, however, was a leader in information services. IBM sold over $10 billion of software each year. IBM also saw much to gain with Java. IBM saw the opportunity to write software once, and have it run on all IBM systems. IBM saw major software and service opportunities. Soon IBM had more Java programmers employed than Sun, or any other company.

Java presented a dilemma to Microsoft. Microsoft owned the most profitable platform in the history of computing — Microsoft Windows. Microsoft recognized the many advantages of having applications written specifically to Microsoft Windows, rather than to a universal platform like Java. It was clear to Microsoft that Sun was the enemy, trying to use Java to displace the Windows platform with a new platform based on Java.

Bill Gates, Steve Ballmer, and other executives at Microsoft were excellent students of history. Historically, the leader of one technology platform fails to be the leader of the next platform. IBM was the mainframe leader. With minicomputers, Digital Equipment displaced IBM's leadership. With personal computers, Compaq displaced Digital Equipment, and ultimately bought Digital. What really displaced the minicomputer was not the hardware of Compaq; it was the software from Microsoft.

With the popularity of the Internet and Java, Microsoft was not going to be delegated to a chapter in business history. Microsoft decided to embrace Internet technology, enhance it, and then put Microsoft in an Internet leadership position. Ditto with Java. Microsoft licensed Java, giving Sun a check for $5 million. Microsoft included Java in the Microsoft Internet Explorer and Microsoft software development kit. As Microsoft proceeded to enhance Java, Sun cried "foul" and a lawsuit ensued.

The battle between Microsoft and Sun has now shifted to new and higher grounds. Sun has made Java part of "SunOne." Microsoft is evangelizing ".Net." Billions are being spent. Customers and partners are being enlisted. Many will use both. The battle will be intense, and continually moved to different grounds, as the players battle for market leadership.

One Billion and Growing

Over one billion people now use Java. Java runs on virtually all computers, and computer operating systems. When you use the Internet, you probably use Java without even knowing that you use it. Applications on your palm computer and cell phone may be written in Java. If you are a smart card user in Europe, Java may even be running on the card. Check your kid's games. Many are written in Java. The revolution continues. Java has changed the world.

A few bright people, with the right strategy, can change the world. So it went with Java, starting with a few bright engineers from "Sun Microsystems Laboratories – not your average tanning salon."

Product Launch

Thirty days from now your career moves forward and your income goes up, or you start looking for a new job. This is a major product launch. It is at the biggest trade show of the year. Rumors are flying about how your toughest competitor is going to preempt you. Your customers have been waiting. Their patience is gone. Your sales partners are restless.

The introduction of a new product touches everyone in a company. It deeply involves those who create the new product. It involves manufacturing and operations. It involves financial and administrative people. Products are brought to market by sales and marketing people.

Successful new product introductions implement the marketing and selling partner strategies, which are detailed in this book. For this reason, we start here. Increasingly, the launch involves new services: information services, financial services, health care, training programs, consulting, outsourcing, and other services. Services are created, given brand names, marketed, sold, and used by customers.

When a new product or service is introduced, the customers take charge. They vote with their money. If you create a better solution for customer needs, sales accelerate. Over time, you can progress from being first to market, to being the market share leader.

Not only are customers voting with their money, so are all the people in the middle who sell and support your product. You must also meet the needs of your channel partners.

What is a Channel Partner?

Channels of distribution are the networks of companies who resell your products and services. Large companies often have complex channels of distribution including distributors between the company and specialized resellers. Each member of your channel is referred to as a channel partner. They include retailers, resellers, wholesalers, solution integrators, strategic allies, and others.

82% of the executives interviewed by Accenture identified channel partners as their prime vehicle for growth. In this survey, $40 trillion is the expected revenue growth through channels between 2000 and 2004.

Got a Light?

People are trying to keep the lights on. Literally. In many parts of the world, the local power utility cannot deliver power 24 hours per day, 7 days per week (24/7). Half the people on this planet cannot get any electricity from a local power utility.

Microturbines are a solution. A midsize business can get all its power by installing a microturbine. In 1998, a little company called Capstone Turbine won the race to be first to market. In 2000, they took their stock public. They beat giants like Honeywell and Siemens. They caught General Electric (GE) off-guard, even though GE is the world leader in power turbines.

How did Capstone do it? First, they had a vision of changing the world. They had a just cause—powering homes and vehicles in a way that dramatically reduced their contribution to global warming. They were flexible. Capstone got prototypes to market, learned, failed fast, and kept making products better. Even though their potential markets were enormous, they started by targeting specific applications. As they say in the Air Force: "They flew under the radar." The big competitors did not see them coming, until Capstone was first to market.

The Capstone team created its own luck. They got the attention of some very smart, and very wealthy investors. Ben Rosen, the financial founder of Compaq (now merged with Hewlett-Packard), was an early investor in Capstone, and joined their Board of Directors. Later, Microsoft founders Bill Gates and Paul Allen invested. The top venture capitalists in the energy field also invested, bringing money, advice, contacts, and additions to the management team.

Like many hot start-ups, Capstone lived off government-funded research projects for years. When Ben Rosen got involved, they targeted turbine-powered clean cars as their first big area of commercialization. In the automotive industry, however, barriers to entry are high. Changing an entire value-chain of suppliers, manufacturers, dealers and service stations is a trillion-dollar proposition. Capstone eventually achieved some success with turbine-powered buses. They were also wise enough to refocus.

In 1997, it was not clear who would be first to market. It could have been any number of giant companies who had more money, people and technology, such as Honeywell's Allied Signal, Ingersoll-Rand, Pratt & Whitney, Toyota, Mitsubishi, and Williams.

Surprisingly, small companies often beat the giants by being first in introducing disruptive technology. For example, Honeywell has well defined processes to develop new products. They carefully evaluate opportunities; form project teams, divide their best engineers between different projects, create committees, create evaluation gates for projects. Large companies also create bureaucracy.

Capstone's CEO, Dr. Ake Almgren, takes a different approach: "When you think you are fast, you need to be faster. Grab an opportunity and respond quickly." Capstone put a few bright engineers in the same room, so they could easily collaborate as they worked through the complexities of building a reliable generator that spins 96,000 times per minute. The designers of engines could work closely with designers of power electronics. Capstone did not slow the process with bureaucracy. They were too small for the usual obstacle course of committees and gates. Honeywell moved too slowly by over-engineering a larger turbine. Capstone won the first battle. Will they win the war?

When a corporation is first to market, the firm should focus on a customer community where there is a compelling problem and low competitive barriers. A customer community is a group of potential customers with similar characteristics. Customer communities are often divided by geography, type of business, and customer needs.

Capstone saw opportunity everywhere, and indeed there was. With each new investor, each new strategic partner, each order from a major customer, they were pulled them in a different direction. Capstone was first to market in a number of segments: Hybrid electric vehicles (HEV); peak shaving; resource recovery in oil fields; resource recovery in landfills; cogeneration with fuel cells; and cogeneration in conventional power plants.

With the Internet boom, Capstone targeted digital power. Computer data centers and high-tech manufacturing needed reliable power 99.999% of the time. No drops, no spikes. Energy from the grid was not good enough. Capstone fit the need perfectly. When the lights went out in California, they targeted standby power.

Capstone attracted great investment partners, and excellent energy partners. The United States Department of Energy awarded Capstone a $10 million research grant.

Press releases were issued about strategic partnerships with several billion dollar energy service providers: NiSource, Cinergy, and Williams. These reseller partnerships promised giving Capstone the ability to accelerate its growth by having giants who could sell, install, and support their microturbines. Unfortunately, the orders promised in glowing press releases did not always materialize. In the following chapters in this book, you will see how press releases are easy, while developing lasting channel partnerships are challenging. You will learn how to build partnerships that grow and endure.

Capstone's first success was close to home. As they attracted the funds to increase their hiring, they expanded throughout the United States. International distributors are important to Capstone as they expand in the Americas, Europe, Mid-East and Asia. International distributors provide years of experience, relationships, teams of sales and technical people and a deep understanding of how business is done in their own country.

Customer Community Leadership

✓ **Being first to market is no guarantee of being the market share leader. Market share dominance must be achieved one customer community at a time. In Chapter 3 of this book, we will look at this strategy in detail.**

Unfortunately, Capstone was unable to maintain their earlier, high-flying successes. In 2001, Capstone went from shipping 421 units one quarter to only 80 the next. Wall Street became skeptical about Capstone's survival. They were losing money so fast that they would burn through their cash in five quarters, unless Capstone returned to selling hundreds of units each quarter.

Capstone encountered problems almost universal in startups — they chased too many market segments at once, and they established more channel partnerships than they could support. To own market segments, customer problems must be solved in detail. It is best to start with only a few channel partners who can take products, like microturbines, and make them part of a complete solutions. Dr. Almgren describes Capstone's current strategy:

> *The microturbine holds the promise to be lower in cost than the incumbent technology, the reciprocating engine, at similar production quantities. We can achieve lower cost by gradually coming down the cost curve with growing quantities. Clayton Christensen identified that for any disruptive technology, the key to growing volume is to first address the unique value propositions for the new technology, before addressing mainstream*

applications dominated by the incumbent technology. At Capstone, our primary focus is on combined heat and power.

Capstone focused on combined heat and power (CHP) in Japan, where energy is expensive and environmental regulations are high. Capstone partnered with the Takuma, the world leader in system integration for recycling, incineration, and water-treatment facilities. Capstone also partnered with Meiden Sumitomo in micro co-generation. Co-generation can take advantage of heat from industrial processes, run the heat through a turbine, and produce power. In the long run, Capstone must effectively partner with these giant energy service providers. Customers ultimately want the convenience, solutions, financial, and service options offered by their long-time energy providers.

With a renewed focus on CHP, Capstone secured a ten-year strategic contract with United Technologies (UTC). UTC owns Carrier, the world leader in heating and air conditioning. UTC also has sold more fuel cells than any other corporation. With a major CHP partner, Capstone's prospects are looking brighter.

The battle is far from over. Honeywell missed being first to market. Honeywell missed being first to 1,000 units, when Capstone outsold them ten to one. Honeywell sold its struggling microturbine business to General Electric (GE). By focusing on a market segment where Capstone is weak, GE could dominate that, and then move to related markets. GE can change the rules. Just as the microturbine disrupted the market for engines and for large turbines, the fuel cell can disrupt the market for microturbines. You may have guessed: GE is developing fuel cells; Capstone is partnering with fuel cell companies.

Channel Partners

Every industry has different types of channel partners. In every industry they go by different names. A major part of success is using the right partners at the right time. We will detail these partner types and the best strategies in future chapters.

Here are some of the channel partner types used by Capstone. Direct sales are used by Capstone to effectively introduce new products, and to explore new markets. Top customers expect executives working for Capstone to deal directly with their company. Development partners, such as the U.S. Department of Energy (DOE) provide Capstone with money, technology and credibility. The DOE is not a traditional reseller; DOE is a strategic ally.

Service providers, such as NiSource, resell the microturbines, and add value. In other industries, they might be called value-added resellers, or solution integrators. They provide a small company like Capstone with "feet on the street." These energy providers have thousands of established customers already buying energy solutions. NiSource can sell, install, and support the Capstone turbines. With these channel partners, Capstone instantly is exposed to thousands of potential customers, without having to add a huge payroll of sales and technical personnel.

E-Bus is an OEM partner. OEM is shorthand for "Original Equipment Manufacturer." E-Bus builds Capstone turbines into buses. The turbine is an invisible part of a total product. E-Bus in an OEM partner of Capstone, just as Dell is an OEM partner of Intel.

Meiden Sumitomo is an international distributor for Capstone. They are an important to Capstone not only because of its trusting customer relationships in Japan, but because Sumitomo adds value by implementing complete systems that provide power and heat. International distributors help companies expand rapidly. They bring valuable customer contacts. They create solutions appropriate to one or several countries. They speak the language.

Strategies for Market Leadership and Expansion with Channel Partners

✓ **Capstone Turbine illustrates how selecting the right strategies, market segments, and partners can lead to early product success. They show us how to be first to market.**

The ultimate winners in distributed power technology are likely to be the companies that best enable customers to buy solutions in the way that they prefer to buy. Early customers wanted to deal directly with Capstone, and take a strong voice in the product design. Mainstream customers now want to buy from companies in the middle (channel partners) that make Capstone microturbines part of more complete solutions that included fuel delivery, use of heat and energy, and integration with other products. Large companies who repeatedly buy from Capstone in volume would want the convenience and efficiency of eCommerce.

Capstone must carefully build global distribution channels and strategic allies. Some of these alliances could become Capstone's fiercest competitors. For example, Cummins supplies the critical components for Capstone. In the future, it could be Capstone's toughest competitor. Fuel Cell Energy partners with Capstone to create a breakthrough cogeneration solution. In the future however, Capstone and Fuel Cell Energy will be fighting for the same business. Integrated providers of natural gas like Dynegy and Williams will continually evaluate whether to partner or compete with microturbine leaders.

Capstone will need to continue to expand its sales in one market segment, and then the next. Because energy is a trillion dollar industry, Capstone will need to deal with increasingly aggressive competitive attacks from companies like Caterpillar, General Electric, and Siemens.

How does CEO Dr. Almgren feel about competing with these giants?: "Large competitors are like aircraft carriers. They have enormous firepower once they are in position. Being a small company, we can win by being like a submarine that moves faster, quickly focuses on targets, and remains invisible until the first strike."

Summary

Be the best for groups of customers. Focus on specific customer communities, products, and services that better match their specific needs. Partners can be engaged in order to develop solutions for these customer communities.

When a new product is based on disruptive technology, customer community leadership is the only way to succeed. Products are not enough; complete solutions must be formed. Leadership begins by being first to market. Achieving dominance in specific market segments accelerates leadership.

In the next chapter, you will see how leadership is sustained with a consistent value discipline. Cost, creative, and customer intimate leadership will be described.

Executive Action

➢ With new products, be first to market.

➢ Expand from one market segment to related segments until you are the market share leader.

➢ Introduce breakthrough products first to a market segment with a compelling need and low competitive barriers.

Sales Action

➢ Understand the total solution needs of your top customers.

➢ If your product is disruptive, focus on a few customers with compelling needs. Only involve channel partners who integrate solutions.

➢ If your competitor is first to market, protect your customers and partners by offering a range of services not available from the innovator.

2

Leadership

Leadership is accomplished by achieving better long-term customer relationships than your competition.

Different customers have different values. One customer may select a restaurant that can feed her daughter's soccer team at a modest cost and with efficiency. Another customer wants to impress a close friend at an elegant restaurant where they will receive outstanding service from the captain, waiter, and wine steward. A third customer wants unique food in a unique setting. Respectively, these three customers wanted Cost, Customer Intimate, and Creative leaders.

✓ **You do not achieve greatness by trying to be all things to all people. The greatest corporations have the courage to be leaders with a business model optimized to Cost, Customer Intimate, or Creative leadership.**

Competitive Strategy, by Michael Porter, shows that competitive advantage is the result of executing a strategy of cost leadership, differentiation, or focus. *The Discipline of Market Leaders,* by Michael Treacy and Fred Wiersema, discusses the following as value disciplines: Operational efficiency, customer intimacy, and product leadership. To make a memorable "3C" model, we will look at these value disciplines: Cost, Customer Intimate, and Creative leadership.

Creative Leaders

✓ **Creative leaders develop breakthrough products and services. They often have a free-spirited corporate culture that encourages innovation. Creative leaders often have complex sales and channel strategies.**

In the early stages of a new product, they need close relationships with customers. Creative leaders take a team approach to selling, with engineers dealing directly with engineers, while sales executives deal with visionary customer executives. As product sales increase, creative leaders need to shift much of their sales to channel partners who are customer intimate leaders or creative leaders. If a product becomes a best seller, then channel partners who are cost leaders become important.

The information technology industry has classic examples of those that succeed by focusing on one discipline. Sun Microsystems made Java a platform by encouraging engineers and all people to be creative. Sun's CEO, Scott McNealy exemplifies this by saying: "To ask permission is to seek denial." Sun is a Creative leader.

Cost Leaders

✓ **Cost leaders drive efficiency and drive down sales cost. Cost leaders do the best job of saving their customers money with lower-cost products and by doing work for their customers. Cost leaders tend to be very-efficient, multi- billion-dollar firms. They achieve economies of scale. Cost leaders invest more in "inside salespeople" who work in call centers, than in more expensive "outside salespeople" who travel to be face-to-face with their customers. Cost leaders are the most aggressive in doing eCommerce.**

Ingram Micro controls over $25 billion of product sales annually, as the world's leading distributor. Technology giants, such as Microsoft and Hewlett-Packard (HP) court Ingram. Ingram is extremely successful at controlling cost. They take orders into the night, configure from an inventory of over 100,000 distinct items, and often ship that same night. They have the technology and business processes to drive their total sales and administrative expenses to less than four percent of sales, holding a distinct competitive advantage. Ingram is a Cost leader.

Cost leaders are excellent in the middle. They are great wholesalers, distributors, financiers, and logistic suppliers. Cost leaders have mottos similar to UPS: "We run the tightest ship in the business." Cost leaders drive payroll costs down.

Customer Intimate Leaders

✓ **The motto of a Customer Intimate leader is "The customer is always right." Customer Intimate leaders are in the people business. They are excellent at being responsive to the unique needs of each customer. Customer Intimate leaders are most willing to invest in face-to-face sales, rather than less expensive "inside sales" call centers and eCommerce.**

A Customer Intimate leader would rather have an Internet site that is wonderful in customer support and training, than a site that is built around promotions and order-taking. Customer Intimate leaders drive payroll cost up. They invest in people.

SAIC is a good example of being a Customer Intimate leader. SAIC is the nation's largest employee-owned research and engineering company, providing information technology and systems integration products and services to government and commercial customers. SAIC scientists and engineers provide complex technical solutions in telecommunications, national security, health care, transportation, energy, the environment, and financial services. SAIC revenues exceed $6 billion per year.

SAIC gets deeply involved with a few customers. They might secure a ten-year billion-dollar contract that involves SAIC putting a team of people on-site at the customer. Customers often treat SAIC people just like their own employees. SAIC is about relationships and being deeply involved in the success of its customers. SAIC is a Customer Intimate leader.

Confused

✓ **Most companies say that they aspire to be leaders in all three disciplines: Cost, Creative and Customer Intimate. Because each leadership model requires different values and financial models, companies that try to be all things to all people end-up in the fourth "C" category — Confused.**

Confused companies say that the customer is always right, then control cost to the point where the customer gets a frustrating series of voice menus, instead of a helpful person on the phone. Confused companies talk about employee empowerment, then discard product and service breakthrough ideas by saying "that's not how we do business here."

Having lost sight of our objectives, we redoubled our efforts.

—Motto of a Confused Company

Sun Microsystems, Ingram, and SAIC are excellent leaders with completely different business models. Ingram generates double the revenue of Sun, with half the employees. In turn, Sun generates double the revenue of SAIC with about the same number of employees. Sun provides great products. SAIC provides great people.

Could Sun be both Creative and Cost leader? Sun could be OK at both. Sun could not be great at both. To be the leader in product innovations such as Internet and Java technology, Sun invests over ten percent of sales in research and development alone. In the middle of a major technology financial recession in 2001 and 2002, Sun Microsystems increased it's spending on research and development

41

(R&D). Only a Creative leader can afford such heavy R&D investments. Sun cannot hold total expenses to less than four percent, as does Ingram. Sun cannot be a creative and a cost leader.

Both companies achieve greatness by optimizing to one business model. In fact, Sun is wise enough to have Ingram distribute some of its products. Ingram can handle distribution better and at lower cost than Sun.

Compaq (now merged with Hewlett-Packard) started by being a creative leader. Rod Canion, and a team of engineers from Texas Instruments, designed the world's best portable computer. The first design was done on a napkin in a restaurant. Compaq stayed focused on being creative. It packed in more features as it reduced weight. It did not try to be low-cost. By being focused on its leadership model, Compaq achieved record growth in becoming a Fortune 500 company in less than five years.

Compaq executed an excellent channel strategy. It sold all products through computer resellers. These channel partners provided customers with support and system integration. Value-added resellers could be customer-focused in a way that Compaq could not.

When Cost-Leader Dell started taking market share from Compaq, alarms went off. Compaq's board replaced Canion with Eckard Pfeifer. The aggressive new CEO waged war on all fronts. Channels were expanded. Aggressive product-pricing was implemented. Compaq tried to be both a Creative and a Cost leader. Many channel partners would compete for the same business driving down their profit margins. It became dangerous for a channel partner to be loyal to Compaq.

To fight Dell, Compaq tried to buy Gateway, another company who was fighting to be the cost leader. Gateway sold directly to customers through telemarketing, and through the Internet. Compaq's channel partners threatened to revolt over the Gateway acquisition. Rather than bet the company, Pfeifer decided not to buy Gateway. Instead he bought Tandem and Digital Equipment. This gave Compaq a global major account sales force selling directly to customers. More importantly, it made Compaq one of the top solution integrators in the world. Solution integration is a Customer Intimate business.

Compaq had lost its way. Trying to be cost, creative and customer intimate, it became confused. Compaq lost money. Its CEO, Pfeifer lost his job.

Compaq's new CEO, Michael Capellas, stated his strategy when he got promoted to the top job: "We want to take major accounts direct (not through channel partners), but a lot of (small and midsize business) customers want value-added people to support them. The goal was to ultimately reach a 40% direct model."

Compaq is now part of Hewlett-Packard (HP); HP continues the struggle for value leadership. Some HP founders and Wall Street investors are concerned about the wisdom of the merger. Investors and customers want to see a company with a clear leadership model. The goal of having 40% of sales through a direct force, and 60% through channels, will work if HP clearly focuses on customer intimate leadership. Customer intimate leadership would also exploit HP's strength in solution integration and services.

How to Fix a Confused Company

✓ **When a company becomes confused, it must refocus on one leadership model. The best path is often to focus on being a customer intimate leader. First some triage may be necessary, including shedding of marginal market segments and marginal customers.**

Creative leaders are challenged to again be creative leaders, because a competitor is now the market share leader. If that competitor is the platform for an entire value-chain, it is especially difficult to again be a creative leader.

It is difficult to refocus on being a cost-leader. Cost leaders operate on thin profit margins. There is no room for the fat R&D, expensive sales, and marketing that confused companies often have.

Ericsson was the largest maker of wireless communications switches and cell phones. Internally some managers wanted it to be the creative leader in third-generation (3G) technology. Others wanted it to be Customer Intimate, building custom networks for large telecommunication firms, the way it had with earlier radio technology. Under the assault of competition for Nokia, Motorola, and other competition, others pushed for Ericsson to gain market share by focusing on cost. Ericsson was confused.

Ericsson is now refocusing on being a customer intimate leader. This is the best strategy. With 85,000 employees and operations in 140 countries, Ericsson needed triage and customer focus. It reduced cost and risk by outsourcing its handset production and merging its mobile-phone operations in a joint venture with Sony.

Even with revenues of $25 billion, Ericsson put a major focus on five customers. It reorganized and formed global customer units for five large European customers: Vodafone Group, France Telecom, Deutsche Telekom, Telefonica, and Telecom Italia Mobile. Ericsson focused on the custom services and large switch specialized options that these customers desire.

Confused Strategy: How it Becomes Policy

Psychobiologists performed a study of our primate cousins. The results show us how corporate behavior really works. Put five apes in a room. Hang a banana from the ceiling and place a ladder underneath the banana. The banana is only reachable by climbing the ladder. Have it set up so any time an ape starts to climb the ladder, the whole room is sprayed with ice-cold water. In a short time, all the apes will learn not to climb the ladder.

Next, take one ape out and replace him with another one (ape 6). Then disable the sprayer. The new ape will start to climb the ladder and will be attacked unmercifully by the other 4 apes. He will have no idea why he was attacked. Replace another of the original apes with a new one and the same thing will happen, with ape 6 doing the most hitting.

Continue this pattern until all the original apes have been replaced. Now all of the apes will stay off the ladder, attacking any ape that attempts to, and have absolutely no idea why they are doing it. This is how company policy and culture is formed.

Wall Street Meets Silicon Valley

A trillion dollars is a lot of money. There are hundreds of trillions of dollars of securities traded each year. As stockbrokers, banks, and insurance companies move on to each other's turf, competition becomes increasingly intense. There will be room for many Customer Intimate leaders, because they can target different market niches and customer groups. There will be one to three big winners in the battle for cost leader, and hundreds of losers. The cost leader in financial services will have billions in capital and invest hundreds of millions in technology in the competition to meet customer needs for lower fees and higher interest rates. An examination of the strategies of several financial service firms reveals different types of successes.

E*Trade has invested heavily in pushing the envelop with advertising, technology, and new business models. In many ways, E*Trade pursued a creative leadership strategy. It also has offered trading for $5 per transaction, the model of a cost leader. It has been aggressive in using online trading and services to take business first from stockbrokers, and then from banks. The average E*Trade customer is someone age 39, with modest assets.

Merrill Lynch is a Customer Intimate leader. Account executives focus on providing personal

46

attention to their customers. Their focus is long-term, not day trading. They want to help their customers manage their wealth, and protect it. Merrill's average customer is 52 years old, with $200,000 in assets. Merrill Lynch has $1.4 trillion customer assets under management, more than all online brokers put together.

In 1998, Merrill stated that the Internet was bad for investors. In 1999, under intense competitive pressure, Merrill bought an online firm, and established a website for all customers. Merrill Lynch has had enough of the competition's in-your-face ads, the lost business, and the pressure to reduce fees. As a Customer Intimate leader, Merrill Lynch now uses the Internet to provide quality customer service. It does not compete on cost per transaction. Rather than play "me too" in trying to catch-up with Internet leaders like E*Trade and Schwab, Merrill is focused on providing top quality personal service to wealthy investors.

Charles Schwab is a Customer Intimate leader success story. They were early in putting brokers on straight salary, to remove the temptation to churn accounts. They were early in offering significant discounts over traditional firms, but they have never tried to be lowest cost. Many Schwab customers prefer the flexibility of online trading, plus being able to talk to a competent person when needed. Schwab is investing millions in both unique online services, and unique branch offices that bring them closer to their customers. Schwab's preferred customers have access to dedicated account teams, who know their customers, and watch out for them. Schwab makes professional research available to their customers online.

As stockbrokers, banks and insurance companies move on to each other's turf, competition becomes intense. There is room for many customer intimate leaders, because they can target different market niches and customer groups. There will be one to three big winners in the battle for cost leader, and hundreds of losers. The cost leader in financial services will have billions in capital and invest hundreds of millions in technology in the competition to meet customer needs for lower fees and higher interest rates.

Summary

Cost leaders do the best job of saving customers money. These leaders also improve quality to lower production cost, to lower the cost of returned goods, and to keep customers for life. Cost leaders are often efficient, multi- billion-dollar global firms.

Creative leaders invest in research and development to ensure a stream of breakthrough products. These leaders innovate to better meet customer needs, and to anticipate future needs.

Customer Intimate leaders differentiate themselves by services designed to meet the unique needs of each customer. These leaders are in the people business.

Your channel partners are a mix of Customer Intimate leaders, Creative leaders, Cost leaders, and Confused leaders. Rethink the need to have a relationship with confused partners. Engage the leaders in the value-discipline in which they are excellent. Do not ask a Customer Intimate leader to run an end-of-quarter discount sale. Do not ask a cost leader to invest in expensive customer intimate services. In Chapter 4, we will see how to focus the coverage of these different partner-types.

Market leadership results from value-discipline leadership and in providing the best products and services for customer communities. In the next chapter, we will examine how corporations progress from one customer community to the next, until market dominance is achieved.

Executive Action

➢ Determine whether your company is a Cost, Customer, or Creative Leader.

➢ If you are a Cost Leader, invest more heavily in "inside sales people." Invest aggressively in eCommerce. Run a tight ship.

➢ If you are a Customer Intimate leader, invest more heavily in major account customer teams lead by senior sales and service people.

➢ If you are a Creative Leader, invest heavily in introducing unique products and services faster than your competition. Run a loose ship.

Sales Action

➢ In customer meetings, focus on the areas where your company is the leader.

➢ If you sell for a Creative Leader, work with channel partners who are Customer Intimate and Creative leaders until the product sells in high volume.

➢ If you sell for a Cost Leader, use eCommerce and volume distribution to free your sales time.

➢ If you sell for a Customer Intimate Leader, get deeply involved with a few customers.

3

Customer Communities to Market Dominance

> **Successful corporations focus on one customer community until they have the #1 share in that community. Then they expand into a related community.**

✓ The best companies avoid attacking a major competitor on all fronts. Leaders divide a large market into customer communities. They focus on a customer community until they have the number one share in that segment. Leaders then take their success to a related customer community. With time, they achieve leadership in the new segment. Corporate leaders expand customer community by customer community until they are established in the broader market.

A customer community is also referred to as a market segment. The idea is to look deeply at the needs of groups of similar customers. When someone at headquarters looks at the entire market, they miss important needs of customers. When we segment, more specific customer needs surface. Improved market research is done by looking into each segment and talking with the industry leaders in each segment. Corporations can offer better services to meet specific customer community needs.

General Electric and Market Dominance

General Electric (GE) is recognized as one of the world's most successful corporations. A strategy that drives this success is that GE accepts nothing less than leadership in any market segment in which it does business. When Jack Welch was promoted to Chairman of GE, he insisted that GE be Number One or Number Two in any market. If you ran a GE business that did not pass the test, you had to "fix, sell, or close" the business.

Before Jack Welch, any business that made appliances was considered a sacred part of GE. When Jack took charge however, GE's central air-conditioning appliance business only had 10% of the market. GE sold the business to Trane, the market leader. Jack was able to take the $135 million from the sale, and invest it where GE could be number one.

Market leaders enjoy many benefits over the competition. Leaders achieve economies of scale. They get the best prices and service from suppliers. Leaders become the industry standard. Cost market leaders improve their cost leadership. Creative market leaders have more to invest in research and development.

Sales and Marketing costs are lower for market leaders. The best, and lowest cost, form of marketing is word-of-mouth. The market leader enjoys the most word-of-mouth exposure. Advertising has a wider reach for market leaders as well. All of these create competitive advantage for the leader, and barriers to other competitors. For example, channel leaders and strategic allies have a strong desire to partner with the market leader for their product area. Unfortunately, if you have a small percentage of the market, attracting good channel partners is hard work.

Even if you are General Electric, you cannot be the leader in all markets. GE was once struggling with a small plastics business that lost money every year. GE could not directly attack larger competitors, such as DuPont, in all markets. When Jack Welch was promoted to run the plastics business earlier in his career, he fought for leadership in one plastics segment at a time, expanding from hair dryers to television sets. It was only later that leadership in automotive and airplane components would be achieved.

How to Achieve Leadership in One Customer Community At a Time

In his must-read book, *Crossing the Chasm*, Geoffrey Moore describes how to succeed in one market segment at a time. He creates the marketing metaphor of a bowling alley, where pins are knocked down in succession. With respect to his inspiration, here is a similar approach:

✓ **Divide a big market into customer communities.**

✓ **Select two dimensions that are important to your business from factors such as geography, industry, application, consumer demographics, and consumer psychographics.**

✓ **Research customer needs.**
✓ **Start where customers have a major unserved need, you face low competitive barriers, and you can add the most value.**
✓ **Have a game plan to expand one segment at a time.**

Leapfrog Enterprises is a leading developer of technology-based learning products for children. In 1995, Mike Wood started with one product, a Phonics Desk®, to help young children with phonics. The next years he added a Phonics Bus® and other "toys" which encouraged learning. In 1998, Leapfrog expanded into teaching math. In 1999, the best-selling LeapPad learning system was launched with interactive books in several learning disciplines.

The following matrix of learning skills and child's age simplifies how Leapfrog expanded from a visionary start-up to revenue rocket growth in the hundreds of millions of revenue. Here, market segments are defined by child age and learning application:

	Reading	Math	Music	Science
Toddler	1	2	4	10
Pre-school	3	5	9	
Elementary	6	8		
Middle school	7			

Leapfrog Enterprises is a prefect name for a company that leaps from success to success from one segment to the next.

BearingPoint

BearingPoint has over 10,000 consultants serving 2500 clients. It was formerly a part of a conservative global CPA firm, KPMG. The consulting group ruffled some feathers when it broke with tradition, spun-off, and took its stock public.

BearingPoint is a customer intimate leader. BearingPoint knows better than to tell its valuable clients "one size fits all." The firm goes deeper into the problems of different customers and different market segments. At a high-level, it looks at the needs of these different markets:

- ✓ **Public Services**
- ✓ **Financial Services**
- ✓ **Communication and Media Firms**
- ✓ **High Technology**
- ✓ **Consumer and Industrial**

BearingPoint offers different services for different markets. High technology companies want help integrating their supply chains. Technology firms introduce new products at ever-faster rates. Healthcare is a large market for technology. A city manager, on the other hand, is concerned about managing funds from many sources. At BearingPoint, segments have different managing partners. They have different specialists. One bank president will tell another bank president to engage BearingPoint. Word of mouth is BearingPoint's best sales tool, and its strongest incentive to keep clients happy.

BearingPoint has grown to over $2 billion per year by providing a variety of services. Some are well-established. Some are improvements of popular client services. Some are new, higher risk, and more likely to catch their competition off-guard. If BearingPoint wants to double its business, it will take a closer look at the needs of each market. In fact, it will examine a number of customer communities with each market. For example, public services could be divided into:

- ✓ **United States Federal Government**
- ✓ **U.S. State Governments**
- ✓ **U.S. Universities**
- ✓ **European Federal Governments**
- ✓ **European Police Departments**
- ✓ **European Universities**

To grow, BearingPoint must create and brand better services. The services must be tailored to customers in a wide-range of market segments. BearingPoint must prioritize these market segments, and focus on its strongest areas, especially when introducing breakthrough approaches. Selectively, it must also risk expanding into new markets.

BearingPoint vs. MarchFirst

BearingPoint was slow to risk expanding into eCommerce and Web design services. MarchFirst came along and aggressively promoted these services to BearingPoint clients. MarchFirst won large multi-million-dollar contracts. Some senior consultants joined MarchFirst to be in a "hot shop."

MarchFirst was the result of the merger of two hot consulting firms, Whittman-Hart and US Web/CKS. With the dot-com explosion, these firms expanded rapidly through mergers to meet the needs of clients racing to do eCommerce. Whittman-Hart provided solutions integration. USWeb/CKS was a leading provider of Internet professional services, with an emphasis on emerging e-commerce companies. They went after all markets and recruited until they had as many consultants as BearingPoint.

If the client wanted a service, MarchFirst offered it. The professional services provided by MarchFirst included business strategy and management consulting, creative branding, marketing, Web application design, software development, packaged software implementation, and network infrastructure design.

In 2000, BearingPoint fought back. KPMG had "spun-off" the consulting business, creating a separate public company, complete with stock options designed to keep their best people. BearingPoint continued to offer improved services in their well-established market segments. They continually improved their ability to integrate complex customer systems. They introduced their own innovative eCommerce and web design services. They did not let these new services outweigh their well-established, highly profitable practices. BearingPoint leveraged their core competencies to do a better job of integrating "front end" web systems with the "back end" systems where they had great expertise.

Who won the battle? BearingPoint. In 2001, MarchFirst went bankrupt. They lost over $7 billion in 2000! MarchFirst lost control by trying to be a creative leader and a customer intimate leader. They failed to balance proven service offerings in established markets with hot new offerings. They were confused.

Microsoft

✓ Achieve market dominance by becoming the platform for an entire industry.

In 1981, IBM selected Microsoft to provide the operating system for the IBM PC. Thousands of software firms, hardware firms and value-added resellers needed a single industry standard for their applications and products. With the IBM endorsement, Microsoft became the favored choice. Microsoft gave developers the tools to port their applications to Microsoft. By doing this, Microsoft built a brand.

Microsoft focused on being the market leader for operating systems. They then used that leadership in operating systems to propel their word processing software ahead of the established leader WordPerfect. Microsoft continued to extend that leadership by moving Excel ahead of spreadsheet leader VisiCalc. Finally, Microsoft solidified its leadership by bundling several applications into Microsoft Office.

Microsoft has been relentless in protecting and expanding its market leadership. It creates momentum and sustains it. The company has achieved market dominance and sustained competitive advantage by becoming a platform for thousands of other products and services. When this happens, the barrier to competition is not simply a firm's product. Instead, the barrier is all the products and services that run on the platform.

A consumer may feel that Linux is a more reliable operating system than Microsoft Windows. However, the consumer needs to run a dozen educational and entertainment applications, which run only on Windows. Microsoft wins.

A corporation may feel that Adobe's Frame is a better word processor than Microsoft Word. However, that corporation must exchange files with other corporations whose people are all trained on Word. Additionally, the firm uses temporary contractors which all know Word. Another win for Microsoft.

Giants such as IBM, Oracle, and Sun have tried to unseat Microsoft's PC leadership. But a frontal assault will not work, because an entire industry is established around the Microsoft platform. To successfully unseat Microsoft, disruptive technology must create a new net services or a wireless platform. New alliances will need to be formed, and market segments must be captured until new leadership is finally achieved.

Summary

The secret to being number one is to start small. Select a customer community where you can do a better job than anyone. Solve a big customer problem that is neglected by your competition. Achieve customer community leadership, and then advance to larger communities until you achieve market dominance.

We have started this book with a section devoted to market leadership. The models developed here apply to your corporation. They also apply to each of your channel partners. Most business is done with channel partners. In the next section, channel strategy will be developed. Then we will see how successful companies put strategy into action.

Executive Action

➤ Identify the customers that generated 80% of last year's profits. Identify the customers that will generate 80% of next year's profits.

➤ Invest in providing improved products and services for the 20% of your customers who deliver 80% of the profits.

➤ Segment the market. Invest in dominating one segment at a time.

➤ Create a plan to make your product family the platform for thousands of products and services provided by other companies.

Sales Action

➤ Select one customer community which has been highly profitable for your firm, and for which your firm offers core advantages.

➤ For your top market segment, join an industry association in that segment. Volunteer to join a committee or their board.

➤ Develop a portfolio of channel partners who cover your targeted market segments.

➤ Use disruptive product announcements to attack competition and changing customer criteria for making decisions.

Part Two

Partner Excellence

4

Channel Strategy

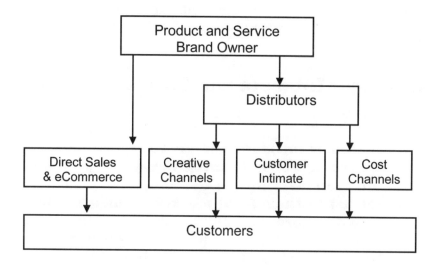

Strategic partners and channels of distribution are critical to the success of most companies. Most sales of products and services are through channel partners. Success involves engaging the correct partners with appropriate customers at the right time. Partners include customer intimate, creative, and cost leaders.

Customer intimate and creative partners provide customers with specialized services, or make your product part of a complete solution. These partners are often best at helping create demand for your products and services in specific markets.

Channel partners who are cost leaders are efficient at fulfilling demand at the right price. They usually resell your products without adding special customer services.

Strategy is driven by several factors: Customer needs, focusing on your strengths, focusing on competitive weaknesses, and having the right mix of sales channels. Successful companies optimize the right mix of partners, direct sales teams, and eCommerce.

Customer Intimate and Creative Partners

✓ **Customer intimate and creative channels are the partners who integrate your products and services into the complete solutions needed in their focal market segments. They provide more complete solutions than you do directly. Your competitors fight with you for the sales focus of these partners. Customer intimate and creative partners are the best channels for products being adapted in specific market segments.**

Information technology (IT) is often sold through customer intimate partners. A computer by itself does not do any good. Its value is in being part of a networked solution, which achieves business goals. Companies often buy networks of computers from solution integrators who take responsibility to make everything work: Computers, network switches, operating systems, databases, and software and application servers. Sales often include consulting and 24/7 services. Solution integrators do not simply fulfill demand. Integrators offer added value.

Solution Integrators (SIs) are often large global firms who generate most of their revenues from professional services. They have recognized names such as EDS, Accenture, Price Waterhouse Coopers, and Computer Sciences. The largest of them all is IBM. Solution integrators may integrate complex systems for a fixed price, or charge by the hour. Sometimes they take full responsibility for running companies' data centers, transfer thousands of the customer's employees to their payroll. The best solution integrators are customer intimate leaders.

Value Added Resellers (VARs) typically generate 20 to 50% of their revenue from services, with the rest coming from the resale of products. They are often focused on market segments such as an industry, an application, a set of suppliers, or geographies. There are thousands of successful VARs.

Oracle is the world's largest database software company. IBM and Microsoft also sell database software. For years, both Microsoft and IBM have been intensely competitive in trying to beat Oracle, and have been consistently unsuccessful in doing so. Oracle uses a wide range of channel partners. One is the OEM channel, which takes core Oracle products and embeds them in other products. The Oracle database engine could be part of a software application for hospitals, lumber yards, streaming video on demand or a HP server appliance.

The best of these OEM partners are creative leaders in their market segments. OEM partners often create larger multi-year sales opportunities. OEM partners often take over one year to evaluate products and design them into their own products. For this reason, revenue often occurs faster from customer intimate partners, than from creative OEM partners.

International distributors often have a very similar business model to VARs. They represent several suppliers of hardware. These channel partners work with their suppliers to have professional consultants and engineers trained on products to a level of certification. They often provide consulting, service and product training to the final customer. Their presence in the country, contacts, and ability to agree to local contract terms often make international distributors the only way to sell products in many parts of the world. They may be allowed to distribute products to other resellers, although global distributors increasingly are handling this now.

Cost Leader Partners

✓ **Cost leader partners allow you to reach a broad global market at a low sales cost. Volume sales result from great products that generate strong customer demand. Cost leader partners tend to efficiently meet demand, rather than create it. However, if you are premature in using cost channels, you will erode profit margins and alienate customer intimate and creative partners, without achieving offsetting benefits.**

Siemens Business Services (SBS) is a large IT cost leader partner. Many corporations prefer to buy everything from SBS including computers, software and networking products, rather than buy directly from the manufacturers. SBS makes it easy to buy all IT products from one source, saving customer-purchasing groups from placing hundreds of separate orders. SBS is an expert at fulfillment as a cost leader.

Direct Sales Teams

✓ **Direct sales usually involve a team from your corporation of account managers, inside sales people, and customer support who work directly with your customers. They work closely with your top global accounts, and provide a direct link to your corporation. Direct sales must be used selectively since it is the most expensive approach.**

Large corporations often use this approach with the 100 largest global customers. Startup firms use direct sales as their main channel as they partner with visionary customers to translate their technology into solutions.

Direct sales coverage has many benefits. A direct account manager can better manage global relationships with a major global account than a local channel partner. A direct sales team can patiently develop and execute a long-range plan with an account. A channel partner tends to be more focused on immediate revenue. A direct team can afford to lose money nurturing a breakthrough product from beta to completion. Channel partners focus on proven products with established market demand.

Use direct teams to cover your most important global accounts. Encourage these teams to only cooperate with partners who add value to these accounts. Do not be afraid of offering large global customers deeper discounts than some of your channel partners. For maximum coverage and profitability, deal with most customers exclusively through channels of distribution.

Sales Coverage Model

✓ **Your decisions about sales coverage are determined by goals about customer satisfaction, market share, revenues, cost, and profit. As we will explore later in this book, your product lifecycle is another factor. Direct sales teams are the most expensive way to support customers. ECommerce is the least expensive.**

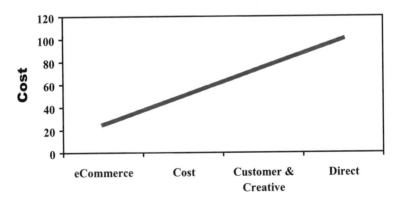

Value to Customer

In the long-term you must maximize profits, not revenue. Customers supported with direct sales will buy more than if their only avenue is cost leader resellers or eCommerce. The gained revenue must be greater than the cost of supporting the customer. Sort your customers by profit potential into four categories:

✓ Direct sales
✓ Customer intimate and creative partners
✓ Cost leader partners
✓ ECommerce only

Market segmentation is a key to successful sales coverage. Start by segmenting your market by product, application, and demographics. Determine the fewest partners that will cover your forecasted channel revenue. Having fewer partners will lower your sales cost. Fewer partners will provide for better profit margins for your partners, and develop their loyalty to you.

The following is a sample, high-level segmentation of a network switch firm. Across the top, we see product lines ranging from simple routers, to complex optical switches. Down the side, we see market segments ranging from the top 100 customers to small business and home markets. Channel coverage includes these: telephone companies (telco), service providers (SP), solution integrators (SI), OEMs that imbed the switches inside their own products, value-added resellers (VAR), software developers, retailers, and direct sales.

Product-Market Segment Strategy
Switch Manufacturer Example

	Routers	Wireless LAN	Voice Recg	Opti Switch
Top 100	3 telco 5 SI 5 OEM	3 telco 5 SI 5 OEM	Direct Only	Direct Only
Mid-size	5 SP 5 SI 400 VAR 5 OEM	5 SP 5 OEM	5 SP Developers	
Small Biz	30 SP 5 OEM 400 VAR	30 SP 5 OEM 400 VAR		
Home	30 SP 100 retailers 5 OEM	30 SP 100 retailers 5 OEM		

The model shows that a volume product, like a router, requires cost leader partners to reach millions of customers. Complex products with disruptive technology, such as voice recognition and optical switches, need to be patiently brought to market by direct sales customer teams.

With this model, the network switch firm can see where it needs to add partners, and where it may need to eliminate excess channel relationships:

Channel partners are the key to sales success in Asia," advises Gigi Wang, CEO of AsiaQuest. Gigi has helped major network switch and other technology firms develop sales and channels in Asia. "Find trusted partners. Take the time to do heavy due diligence, since you will be working with the partners for years. Talk to lots of people before authorizing a partner. Look for partners who complement your products with strong value-added services.

It is tempting to let anyone sell your product. The more, the merrier. Ironically, more resellers does not guarantee more sales. With too many resellers, profit margins shrink for them to the point where they drop you and start selling for your competition. There are a lot of hidden costs in supporting channel sales: People, inventory, logistics, training, marketing, information technology, and so on. In each market segment, the point of maximum profits looks like this graph.

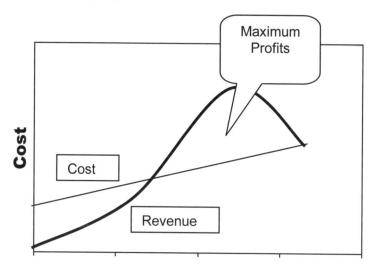

Number of Resellers

Two-tiered or "Not to Tier"

Suppliers of products and services may or may not put distributors between themselves and their channel partners. When they put a distributor or wholesaler in the middle this is called two-tiered distribution. Most technology hardware products use two-tiered sales coverage models. In some industries, large companies have complex channels of multiple layers. This is sometimes called "n-tier" distribution.

Distributors can save you a fortune in inventory costs, capital costs and employee expenses. A distributor could inventory $1 billion for a $10 billion company. The distributor could take orders into the night from thousands of resellers, provide immediate credit, and ship overnight. The supplier sees accelerated revenue, lower inventory cost, no extra capital required to handle credit and leases, and saving the need to hire a number of added people.

Many distributors may court an industry-leading supplier. The supplier may agree to give the distributor an added 10% margin above normal reseller margins. In return, the distributor may agree to dedicate a number of people to the supplier, take a large inventory position, and implement a number of marketing, training, and support programs.

A small supplier may have to offer a distributor an added 15% discount and advance significant money to get the distributor to implement reseller recruiting, training, marketing, and other programs. Even then, the supplier may be too small to get the distributors attention.

When deciding whether to go to a two-tiered distribution, evaluate whether it is profitable. Are the cost savings in outsourcing inventory management, sales, support, and other costs, greater than the revenue lost from deep distributor discounts? Do not be captivated by the distributors size or the number of its resellers. You, not the distributor, will drive end-user demand and channel sales.

Ingram Micro is the largest information technology distributor on earth. They are a cost leader. From over 100 countries, over 170,000 computer resellers can configure systems, place orders at Ingram's secure eCommerce site, talk to a sales or technical person, ask for an expanded credit line, get products shipped, and track the shipment on the Internet. Not only are they often the low-cost distributor for over 280,000 products, they also have the efficiency to lower costs in other ways for their reseller customers.

Tech Data is Ingram's largest competitor. Tech Data is growing faster through global acquisitions, innovative logistics support, and by being responsive to channel partners. Both Ingram and Tech Data represent the best of the two-tiered global distribution system. They do not sell to the final customer. They sell exclusively to resellers. If a distributor competes with its resellers, the distributor loses. Even the perception of competition can create serious problems.

Computer and network solution integrators often prefer to order from Tech Data or Ingram, rather than the separate hardware and software firms represented. A complex solution may require hardware and software from a dozen vendors. In buying from a distributor, they get one-stop shopping, and often with faster delivery.

In the computer field, there was a hybrid model in the USA called an aggregator. Aggregators had one division that acted as a distributor to computer resellers. Another group sold directly to corporate information technology (IT) groups. By competing with their reseller customers, aggregators got into trouble. Wall Street darlings, like Intelligent Electronics (IE), were unable to sustain the hybrid model. Resellers threatened to desert IE. IE bought stock in their key resellers to save the relationship. It did not work. Aggregators disappeared, or wisely transitioned into being either a distributor or corporate reseller, but not both.

This hybrid model is still widely used by international distributors. Because of the channel conflict it creates, the hybrid approach will shrink over time.

The problems with being a hybrid model are now being learned by Reuters, the largest provider of electronic information in the world. Stockbrokers and banks are its largest customers. Reuters owns most of Instinet, which allows stockbrokers to trade stocks around the clock, even when major exchanges are closed.

Instinet alienated its large broker customers, when it did business directly with major institutional accounts, such as mutual funds. Instinet then appeared to compete with broker customers by filing with the SEC plans to offer stock trading, mutual funds, and retirement accounts through a new brokerage firm called *Instinet.com*. Major Reuter's customers such as Schwab, Fidelity, Goldman Sachs, J.P. Morgan Chase, E*Trade, and others retaliated by forming their own electronic communication networks to compete with Instinet.

Complement or Compete

Fierce battles rage inside many companies about whether to protect their channel relationships, or compete directly for business. The Internet has only intensified the debate. It is now easier to reach the final consumer of a product on the worldwide web. A good website can appear more friendly than a reseller with poor product knowledge and selling skills. Financial executives often drive for the cost reductions that can be achieved through bypassing complex two-tiered distribution.

The other side of the argument starts with loyalty to the channel partners who have been critical to past successes. These partners may have personal relationships with the final customers. In many cases, only the partners know who the final customers are. In the end, your product may be worthless unless it is integrated into a complete solution.

Who Has More Power?

✓ **When deciding to sell directly instead of through channels ask: Who has more power, you or the channels?**

It is common for an airline to command up to 80% of the traffic in key airports. Atlanta is a major hub for Delta, Chicago for United, Dallas for American, and so on. Airlines recognized that they have more power than travel agents in hub cities, arguably monopoly power. Airlines sell most of their seats through travel agents. It was common for airlines to pay a ten percent commission to travel agents. Now airlines are systematically reducing travel agent fees, encouraging customers to buy directly through 800 numbers, through their own Internet sites, and other sites like *Orbitz.com* and *Expedia.com*.

By contrast, let us take a manufacturer of home improvement tools. Virtually all the company's business is through 5 national store chains. Home Depot is 60% of the total business. The company has lots of competition. Imagine what would happen if this manufacturer decided to setup its own Internet site selling tools at a deeper discount than customers could buy from Home Depot. Home Depot would drop their line. The manufacturer could go out of business. In this case, the channel partners have more power.

Seeing who has the most power is not always obvious. Multi-billion dollar Johnson and Johnson is the world's largest supplier of hospital supplies. On the surface, it appears to wield more power than a small-town doctor. Yet, when people require knee surgery, it is the doctor who wields the power. The patient is unlikely to surf the Internet, looking for the best deals on artificial knee replacements, and all supplies consumed in the surgery. The surgeon often specifies every thing for the surgery, and the hospital purchases accordingly.

A more complex question is the power relationship between the surgeon, and the company paying the bill. The specified surgical supplies, and the authorization for surgery is often a power struggle between the physician and the payment provider, such as a large insurance company or HMO. Johnson and Johnson must not only consider surgeons as a critical part of its channel model, it must also work closely with payment providers, hospital online procurement systems, and more.

Summary

Different customers and market segments are best served in different ways. When selling complex products to large global account, the customer expects a direct sales team. Customer intimate partners are wonderful for adding unique services that transform your product into complete solutions specific to the needs of customers and specific market segments. Creative leaders are ideal for putting your product inside of their own. Cost leaders allow you to scale quickly to meet the needs of a broad market. When you have a variety of products and services, segment the market, and then focus the partners in the segments for which they are best.

Channel strategy leads to action plans. The next chapter details how to implement strategy and get results.

Executive Action

> ➤ Create a vice president of global channels and alliances, which is a peer to your vice president of global direct accounts.

> ➤ Create a channel coverage model matrix with one dimension, one being products and services, and a second dimension being market segments.

> ➤ Develop and use a comprehensive partner database that includes the partners' value-discipline (remember the 4 Cs) and authorized products.

> ➤ Write a channel business plan including forecasts, goals, strategies, and tactics.

Sales Action

> ➤ For each customer, identify the channel partner, which can best help expand your business.

> ➤ In your personal contact database, add a field for each partner that identifies whether their value-leadership (cost, creative, customer intimate, or confused).

> ➤ Have customer-planning sessions with channel partners.

5

Channel Management

✓ Sales channel executives hold the key to profitability. Corporations want to grow sales revenue and also lower total sales cost. The smart executives will succeed by being effective in each of these areas:

- ✓ Strategy
- ✓ Coverage
- ✓ Mindshare
- ✓ Channel Marketing
- ✓ Partner Relationship Management
- ✓ Teaming
- ✓ Money

Strategy Implementation

Succeed by getting everyone to execute the same strategy. Channel managers get results. They are responsible for achieving revenue targets through channels of distribution. They recruit added channel partners. They fix broken relationships. They terminate partner agreements that cannot be fixed. Channel management starts with the people on the front-line who work with channel partners.

You can succeed if everyone is executing the same strategy. A good strategy includes people at headquarters and people in the field. It includes channel sales, support, marketing, and operations. It includes your channels of distribution.

Avoid the behavior of confused companies where you see one executive group bypassing channels at the same time front-line managers are recruiting more; one group developing a direct marketing promotion, while another group is implementing a competing channel marketing promotion. Confused companies follow this advice:

When you come to a fork in the road, take it.
— **Yogi Berra**

Before you update your channel plan, and do more recruiting, you need to determine your ideal sales coverage model. Only then will you recruit the right partners and deploy the most effective programs.

Coverage

✓ **Sales coverage starts with segmenting the market to see where more partners are needed, and where there are too many.**

Channel management is a constant process of improving strategy and coverage, then recruiting and terminating channel partners that best cover the market segments. When you recruit, you want the best. Over time, you learn which partners get positive results, which relationships can be fixed, and which need to be terminated.

For example, a computer company has 40 resellers in Florida selling to manufacturers. Only 10 are needed. In fact, with the 10 best partners revenue would increase, because reseller profit margins would improve, thus increasing reseller motivation to sell. With only 10 channel partners, training and channel marketing would be concentrated on the best. The company should focus on strengthening business with the top 10, and terminating or refocusing the rest.

The same computer company might also determine that it has no coverage of financial service firms, and decides to recruit the 3 resellers for that market segment, or refocus 3 of the 40 resellers on this neglected segment.

When recruiting, develop a database of potential partners. Secure appointments with the executives of your potential partners. Meet them one-on-one to discuss a long-term alliance. Only win-win relationships will endure and make everyone money. Deeply understand their business. Show them how your partnership meets their key business goals. Develop a team business plan for your mutual success. Sign an agreement.

In your meetings with a potential partner, remember that you need to sell them on why they should commit to doing business with you. In their minds they will be asking questions such as the following: What is our profit margin? Will they bring us customers or cost us customers? Will we need to hire people who are difficult to find? Do they have a great channel program? Will we make millions?

Reality is that most channel partners do not work out. You try to fix these relationships with good business plans, ongoing training, team sales calls, channel marketing, and more. When they do not work out, you can often sit down and discuss the situation. Often agreements are terminated by mutual consent. Your channel agreement should include the right to terminate without cause. Without this, our example of reducing 40 resellers to 10 would become very difficult.

Team Business Plan

Successful partnerships involve communication and plans to achieve specific goals. It is wonderful to declare that you will do a million dollars of business together. The plan shows you "how." A team business plan states what your partner will do and what your organization will do to accomplish stated goals.

Most people skip the plans because plans change. It takes time to create a plan. Most partnerships waste a year of many people's time, because they did not invest a day in deciding how they would succeed together: "First agree on how the channel partner adds value. It is either in services, intellectual property, or logistics," advises Joe Womack, Vice President of Sun Microsystems' multi-billion dollar Central Region. "The relationship can then be built on the partner's core competency. Channel partners must make money. Clearly articulate your company's long-term goals for using channels. A great enemy of channel relationships is uncertainty. Be consistent."

Here is an example of good planning. A regional solution integrator (SI) decides that it wants to sell and support products for a hot storage hardware company. The SI principals meet with the channel management of the storage company. All agree to a goal of one million in annual revenue for the storage products. They agree to target ramping revenue by quarter: $100,000 in quarter one, $200,000 in quarter two, and so on. The SI agrees to target an underserved market: Independent-training companies with large graphic and video libraries. The hardware company agrees to advance $10,000 of marketing funds towards a marketing campaign and trade show participation. The SI agrees to match the $10,000.

In three hours, the channel partner and the product company have created an intelligent plan that will make them both successful. Included are monthly action items, including the names of those responsible. There is investment in both sides. The partnership is created to succeed, not fail.

Some companies make these plans part of their partners' agreements. Good channel managers monitor plans and keep the relationship on track. Annually, executives can be brought together from both sides to plan for greater success in the next year.

A team business plan includes targets for getting specific people trained. It includes channel marketing. It targets appropriate market segments and customers. It gets both sides working together. It sets the stage for the following "mindshare" and channel marketing ideas.

Mindshare

✓ **Mindshare is the amount of time that your channel partners think about your products and services. You want your partners' minds and hearts. Mindshare leads to partner loyalty.**

Your best channel partners have many suitors. They carry hundreds, if not thousands, of products. To get their focus on your products and services, show customer intimate partners how you help them sell their highly profitable services. If you cannot, you need to rethink your channel strategy. Show cost leader partners how they can make money selling in volume. If you cannot, you do not want to have cost leader partners.

Training is a key to mindshare. The ideal training involves a mix of web-based mentored learning, instructor-led seminars, and ongoing collaboration. Certification programs for technical people have been a major component of channel success for companies like Cisco, Oracle, and Microsoft. Your certification training should be so effective that trained people have higher billing-rates and make more money. Training should galvanize sales, and have sales people make presentations and deal with sales case studies.

Ongoing support tailored to channel partners is another key to success. Facilitate Internet collaboration between partners to empower them to solve many of their own problems.

"Channel members are typically quite entrepreneurial. They always look at many options and many vendors. You have their mindshare when you have a disproportionate amount of their entrepreneurial spirit. You have mindshare when they feel a part of your team," Joe Womack. "Vendors should take the first step in building mindshare. Give new partners seed opportunities. Do not wait for them to find the first prospect."

Create enduring mindshare by being the best partner for your channel partners.

Channel Marketing

✓ **Make it easy for partners to spend their money promoting your products.**

Your partners protect and extend your brand. That is one reason that you choose partners carefully. You are known by the company that you keep.

If you want to direct partner activity to specific market segments, do it with a carrot. Provide added marketing funds and easy to implement programs. Be ready to have conference calls and plan team marketing that includes you, them, and other strategic allies. Leverage your funds by co-marketing with strategic allies and partners.

Extend channel marketing to your channel sales people. Do business planning and forecasting with one partner at a time. Your field channel sales and marketing people can then project manage the plan. Use major product launches to get added mindshare and to announce major channel marketing initiatives.

Sun Microsystems wants to continue the high growth of its storage area networks. It increased marketing development funds (MDF) on storage sales to create a special incentive to its channels to focus on storage. It hosted brochures and slide presentations on its channel website targeting different audiences: Executives, technical, service providers, manufacturers, and financial services. Sun prepackaged marketing promotions for channel partners including the following: The ordering of 4-color brochures with the partners name, digital images for various sized ads, telemarketing scripts, approved direct marketing organizations, and prepackaged customer seminars.

Your partner website should make it easy for partners to implement your channel marketing programs and extend your brand.

Partner Relationship Management

✓ **Partner Relationship Management (PRM) allows you to know about your channel partners and their customers. PRM is the strategies, processes, and software applications that allow companies to work closely with their channel partners.**

PRM allows you to automatically distribute information, digital marketing files, and prices to your channels. PRM gives you real-time information about what your channels are marketing, learning, proposing, and selling. PRM also improves channel management in all of these areas:

- ✓ **Channel Marketing**
- ✓ **Channel Sales**
- ✓ **Channel Support**
- ✓ **Channel Efficiency**
- ✓ **Channel Reports and Analysis**

PRM is to partner relationships, as Customer Relationship Management (CRM) is to customer relationships. The best PRM systems integrate with CRM so that everyone in the supply-chain works together in selling and supporting the final customers.

To have your products presented to customers in the best light, you want to either automatically update your partner websites as you make changes, or run sections of your partner sites for them. PRM expert, Philippe Lavie, recommends using PRM to improve all of these:

- ✓ **Channel Communication**
- ✓ **Lead Generation**
- ✓ **Lead Management**
- ✓ **Training**
- ✓ **Demand Fulfillment**
- ✓ **Service Management**
- ✓ **MDF Management**

PRM allows a firm to get detailed information about partner pre-sales, sales, and support. Analysts help manufacturers see which partners are performing, and which are no longer necessary. Analysts can instantly spot sales trends, allowing firms to adjust forecasts, inventory, and promotions.

The best PRM systems provide collaboration that allows groups to communicate with web, email, instant messaging, and voice applications in a way that knowledge is captured and managed.

Hewlett-Packard plans to share customer data with partners through PRM. Once the tools are in place, Hewlett-Packard partners will be able to view service requests, customer requirements, deadlines, and problems. Hewlett-Packard can route sales leads to partners online and track the sale.

3Com increases channel sales by providing a 3Com storefront on each of its channel partners' websites. 3Com's channel partner program, Focus, is powered by PRM applications. 3Com channel partners can quickly set-up an e-Commerce site that includes web-based catalog sales. The system includes e-quoting, e-marketing, eCommerce, and real-time reporting of partner sales to 3Com. 3Com promotions are instantly available on partner web sites. Resellers can easily implement 3Com's latest marketing campaigns.

By helping resellers better manage their own websites; 3Com has more channel partner loyalty. With PRM, 3Com becomes the preferred provider of networking products. 3Com also provides partners with ideas about selling new solutions, product suggestions, promotions and marketing campaigns that can be easily launched from the partner desktop.

Teaming and Managing Channel Conflict

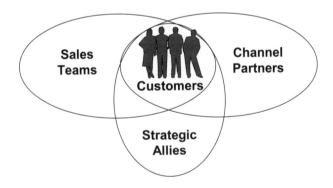

Teaming involves getting a direct sales organization to involve channel partners in sales and implementation. Where it works well, there is wonderful synergy. Where it does not work, there is channel conflict. This conflict is a major challenge for sales executives.

Even the best coverage and compensation models cannot eliminate conflict. As a sales executive you create coverage models that maximize revenue and lifetime customer relationships. You manage conflict by being proactive, and by successfully intervening.

Overlapping sales coverage, compensation, and lack of strategy can all cause conflict. Much conflict comes from DNA. Human DNA is programmed to be territorial. The need for power and control is innate.

Channel managers should frequently be awarded the Congressional Medal of Honor. Where millions of dollars are at stake, conflicts occur, and emotions run high. Channel managers have the responsibility to drive growth, deal with legal issues, enforce contracts, terminate non-performing partners, help good partners resolve problems, and generally try to be in ten places at the same time. Conflicts occur between partners, and between partners and direct sales. In a bid to get extra margin, everyone is constantly campaigning for the special deal.

Channel managers deserve more respect. All too often, what they get are threats, lawsuits, shipping problems, credit problems, and increased revenue goals with decreased marketing budgets. When I was driving 300% annual revenue growth, conflicts were brought to me that frequently started with a string of expletives, then the threat of a lawsuit, then the promise of calling my CEO, and finally a presentation of the problem. No lawsuits were filed, and all issues taken to the CEO returned to my desk, as I gave it my all to mediate conflict and keep growing the business.

Gigi Wang recalled a true experience that occurred while she was building Asia channel marketing for a major network equipment company. She and the company's regional sales manager were at a customer event in the Philippines. The sales manager had made sales calls with channel partner #1 the day before. Now he was engaged in a conversation with the president of a channel partner #2. The president was smiling, but it was very clear, that the sales manager went with the wrong partner to call on a major customer. In no uncertain terms, the president said that the account was his customer. Throughout the conversation, the president's bodyguard kept touching a bulge in his suit that strongly resembled a gun. The sales manager promptly cancelled a scheduled golf game with channel partner #1, and went directly to the airport.

This episode in channel management confirmed the adage that you can win more conflicts with a smile and a gun, than you can with a smile. The episode also confirmed that you should not try to win with a five iron, if the other guy is using a 45mm automatic.

Teaming and managing conflict starts with strategy. Direct sales normally have a high payoff when focused on major global accounts. When your sales people are paid on everything in a territory, then your travel and sales cost can be high. Channels are often the ideal way to cover middle-market, small business, consumers, and international expansion.

Compensation-neutral is an effective way to reduce channel conflict. Pay direct sales people for all business in their assigned accounts regardless of whether they took the order, or whether the order was placed electronically or through a partner. You cannot afford to pay expensive account executives to process routine orders. Do not pay direct sales anything for general territory business where you do not want them focused.

Do not worry about having "zero" conflict. If you have no conflict, you have left a lot of money on the table for your competition. The idea is to dominate accounts and markets, using the most cost-effective channel to ensure customer satisfaction.

An example of "Teaming" would be a software company that has exciting wireless applications for financial service firms. For their solution to be widely deployed, they need partners who can integrate solutions with wireless switches, network integration, database integration, and enterprise software integration. The middle market is 100% managed by channel partners. Therefore, all leads in this market go to the partners.

The software company directly handles 50 large banks. This allows them to get very close to their best customers and tailor the applications to their needs. Initial sales would not have been profitable to the channels. These leading banks also evaluate future technology. Direct sales people can bring solution integrators into these banks, and know they will still receive 100% of their sales commission. There is teaming, not conflict.

Being proactive in the previous example involved assigning 50 large banks to your direct team, and focusing channels on the rest of the world. Further, your discounts in these 50 major banks may exceed the discounts that your partners receive. No one can make a nickel stepping on to another's turf. Therefore, there is no problem. Right? Wrong.

Your biggest customer goes on an acquisition spree, acquiring 20 banks handled by partners for years. The partners tell you to protect them, or they will move the whole bank to your competitor. Now you get to make a successful intervention. You listen carefully to your partners. If you love them, show it. If a reseller has been trouble and unprofitable, you can ignore their threats. You can even discuss going your separate ways.

Successful interventions can require investing some money. You could provide an agent fee of 3% to 5% for business in the 20 acquired banks that you now take direct, for example. You could sometimes subcontract implementation of your services to your partners.

"If you have channels, you have conflict," Joe Womack accurately observes. "You need to build an open, honest, trusting relationship. Rules of engagement must be established. This starts with agreeing to partner with the one who brings the opportunity. During the sales cycle, the customer may want one party, but not the other. There must be an understanding of when to continue working as a team, and when to avoid jeopardizing the sale. 50/50 relationships over the long-term are often a series of 80/20, then 20/80 transactions. It is important to have ongoing communications, and next expect each sale to work perfectly for all parties. Stay focused on building long-term relationships."

Partner Advisory Council

An advisory council can be a powerful way to reduce conflict, improve partner relationships, and get better visibility into your supply chain. There are many effective formats for a council. The idea is to give your best partners a direct voice to your top management. Have meetings that explore everything from your corporate future to tactical issues.

When Carol Bartz took over as CEO for Autodesk, she assembled her top value-added resellers. She asked them to tell her how to fix her new company, and gain market share. When she got some polite discussion, she asked all her executives to leave the room. She then told her partners that she wanted the truth, and encouraged bluntness. She was then given a detailed list of things to fix. She also got a razor sharp picture of what her competition was doing. Carol Bartz used a channel council to give her the data to aggressively counter competition, expand into new areas of design modeling, and build a Fortune 500 company.

If you do not have a channel advisory council, form one. One approach is to invite five to eleven of your best, and most vocal, partners to meet your executives in person. Pick a resort hotel, and pick-up the airfare (if their corporate policy permits it). Encourage them to set the agenda for the day. Encourage them to establish an annual rotation of members. Let them do most of the talking, and take lots of notes.

Legal guidance is always a good idea. This is not a forum for price-fixing or collusion. This is a forum to grow your business. It is an ideal way to treat partners as partners. Channel consultants can be effective in helping you start a council. They can be good at facilitating the first meeting. They can be effective in team building, conflict resolution, or annual "brainstorming" sessions.

Good councils often meet quarterly. Minutes of each meeting are distributed. Action items are taken. Show that you listened. Keep them informed on the status of each action item. Part of the council meeting can involve task groups to focus on customer support, new products, market segments, competition, and more. Monthly conference calls can be added.

Unfortunately, many council meetings lose their effectiveness. The number one reason is lack of progress on action items. Number two is politics. Channel and marketing mangers can be tempted to always look good to top management. They turn council meetings into orchestrated "show and tell." Partners are wined and dined. Regrettably, this way partners are not given the opportunity to discuss the very issues that you need to hear.

Take a deep breath. Trust your partners. Let them run the council meetings. You will gain deep insights into how you can gain permanent competitive advantage with the right products, services, and channel programs.

"Show Me the Money!"

As in the movie, "Jerry Maguire," the battle cry of channel partners is "Show me the money!" Unless everyone is making money, your channel program is not working at its best. Money is the feedback to reevaluate the strategy and tactics discussed in this paper.

Be the platform for your partner's profits. You have their loyalty. They will invest in added people to sell and support your product. They will train them. They will implement your marketing programs. If partner mindshare and sales are below your target, it may be because your direct sales are undercutting your channel-pricing. It could be that you have too many cost leader partners bidding down the street price so that no partners can afford to generate demand for your product.

Partnerships look great in the beginning. Most do not get past the press release. With some of your channels, you will need to discuss the fact that the relationship is not working. With some, the best answer is to agree to terminate the agreement. Create a plan that can be implemented, then implement it.

You have a number of goals: Increasing revenue, customer satisfaction, growing share in targeted market segments, and promoting your most profitable and available products and services. Align your partner sales and support activity with these goals. Smart suppliers can often reduce partner discounts, and offer added incentives to achieve these goals.

For example, you could lower your partner discount from 40% to 20%, and then implement programs that improve your partners' total profits. Partners often make most of their money from services. You could package and brand partner services. Then give them the tools and training to implement these services. Many of Microsoft's best partners make zero from product sales and everything from services.

You could offer fees or bonuses to partners based on customer satisfaction surveys you conduct with their final customer. This is a powerful way to reward the channel partners who add value, and best support the customer.

If you are targeting certain market segments or products, you can offer special marketing funds and promotional kits to focus channel partner efforts.

✓ **Money drives sales channel behavior. Match channel compensation to your corporate goals. Measure what works. Use the results to improve your channel coverage model, your discount and compensation programs.**

Summary

You are on the way to building a Revenue Rocket. Translate strategy into results be progressing through these seven steps. Learn to improve by seeing how profits are optimized for your corporation, your customers, and your partners:

- ✓ **Strategy**
- ✓ **Coverage**
- ✓ **Mindshare**
- ✓ **Channel Marketing**
- ✓ **Partner Relationship Management**
- ✓ **Teaming**
- ✓ **Money**

Channel management centers around partners who resell or receive compensation for the sales of your products and services. In the next chapter, we will see how these principals apply with strategic alliances that may share common goals, but have no interest in a reseller arrangement.

Executive Action

Identify the target number of partners needed in each product category. Recruit and terminate partners to match the targets.

Protect needed partner profit margins.

Create marketing campaigns by product market segment. These can be implemented by your partners with their money.

Implement PRM.

Run quarterly Channel Advisory Council.

Sales Action

Write profiles of the type of partners you now need to drive your channel recruiting.

Plan a customer event and co-marketing campaign with channel partners that focus on your top market segment.

Train the best. Terminate the rest.

Be proactive in identifying and managing conflict (it is part of the job). Listen, summarize the issues, and recommend win-win solutions.

Continually improve channel management by fine-tuning how everyone makes money.

6

Strategic Alliances and Serial Polygamy

> **The fable about the lamb sleeping with the lion was started by the lion's PR firm.**

Strategic alliances can work when complementary firms work together in delivering customer solutions. An alliance is stable and successful when it forms a compelling solution platform for a market segment. Trust is built one person at a time. Partnerships are built on achieving mutual success. Partnerships endure when the strategic goals of the participants are met.

Serial Polygamy

Nowhere in the history of humankind has there been such a history of multiple families being simultaneously married. More shocking is the way the marriages dissolve a few months later being replaced with new marriage partners. Serial Polygamy.

We saw a number of these shotgun weddings with the "dot com" bubble and burst. ECommerce marriages of convenience took place. Marriages are necessary to provide the infrastructure that no one company can provide. In the race to be the leading platform for the new economy, global telecommunication firms partnered with eCommerce software firms who partnered with large data centers who partnered with leading credit card processors. When these partnerships did not make everyone overnight billionaires, disagreements turned into front-page divorces. Former partners became intense competitors: Serial Polygamy.

When Microsoft launched Windows 98, it featured favorite channels where partners could push their content to your desktop, much as television pushes its content to your TV set. One partner was The Walt Disney Company, a global leader with content including favorite movies, cartoons and TV shows. The Walt Disney Company was also important as the owner of ABC broadcasting, ESPN Sports Network, and other TV channels. Microsoft wanted to extend its market share dominance from PCs to TVs. Microsoft anticipated a future where the Internet and TV would converge.

The Microsoft-Disney alliance was a marriage of convenience. Microsoft is determined to be the number one Internet portal, integrating MSN and its other Internet portals. The Walt Disney Company purchased Infoseek, a leading Internet portal to accelerate the creating of *Go.com*. The Walt Disney Company realized that Internet access would move from slow telephone lines, to high bandwidth phone and cable networks. The Internet would offer rich full-motion video, along with easy to navigate menus. The Walt Disney Company Chairman and CEO Michael Eisner correctly stated, "Our content becomes more important as the bandwidth increases."

There was a problem with the partnership. Microsoft and The Walt Disney Company were intense competitors, each aspiring to be the owner and distributor of the world's most valuable digital content. Their marriage ended. Serial polygamy.

AOL and Microsoft

AOL Time Warner gives more people access to the Internet than Microsoft. AOL has a unique audience of over 40 million. Microsoft partnered with AOL in the battle of the browsers. Netscape had market dominance of Internet browsers. Microsoft wanted to be the leader. Microsoft formed an alliance with AOL. AOL offered the Microsoft Internet Explorer as its preferred browser. In return, Microsoft featured AOL Internet access on every copy of Windows 98 shipped.

AOL Time Warner increasingly recognized that Microsoft had relentless ambitions to replace AOL as the most popular portal to access the Internet. AOL bought Netscape. The Microsoft-AOL divorce ended in court with AOL Chairman Steve Case giving testimony in the Microsoft anti-trust suit. Serial Polygamy.

"Only the Paranoid Survive"

Only the Paranoid Survive is an excellent book by Dr. Andy Grove, the former CEO of Intel. The title is fitting for this brilliant man who escaped Hungary in 1956, supported himself while earning a PhD in physics, then advanced at Intel, finally becoming CEO and Chairman of one of the most admired companies on the planet. It is invariable hard to compete against Intel, one of the world's most feared companies.

Dr. Grove and the Intel team have built the most successful semiconductor manufacturer of all time by being paranoid, courageous, responsive, ruthless, and brilliant. Intel was a small manufacturer of computer memory. With their "paranoid" radar, they anticipated intense price competition from Asian semiconductor giants in memory chips. Intel bravely exited the memory business, and focused on microprocessors.

Intel has been courageous and ruthless in becoming dominant in microprocessors. Motorola was once much larger than Intel, but Intel was relentless in pursuing design-wins for new computers and other devices. Now Intel is the giant.

Intel constantly anticipates competitive attacks from the global giants, and surprising newcomers. If AMD tries to leapfrog Intel, Intel changes the rules of the game. If graphics become important, then Intel becomes the graphics leader. If palm devices look like a threat, Intel buys ARM technology to take a lead in the palm area. If Transmeta targets low-power consumption, Intel beats them to market with a low-power chip that runs current applications.

A key to Intel's success is their partnership with Microsoft. Both are known as ruthless competitors. Both will work very hard to make a partnership a success, as long as it is in both of their best interests. Intel and Microsoft have a strategic alliance that created the dominant platform for personal computing.

IBM brought Intel and Microsoft together in 1981, when the IBM PC became the industry standard. Thousands of software firms, hardware firms and value-added resellers needed a single industry standard for their applications and products. That standard was Intel-Microsoft. It still is. An entire multi-billion dollar value-chain depends on Intel and Microsoft staying married. The most successful strategic alliances become platforms for an entire industry.

Intel and Microsoft have worked for over 20 years to ensure that their alliance is successful. Top executives meet, strategize, and work through conflicts. Collaboration is constant through product development lifecycles to ensure compatibility. Hundreds of millions are spent in co-marketing their products. They share common channels of distribution.

They usually avoid competing with each other. For the most part, Intel does hardware. Microsoft does software. There is a major exception to the non-professional, competitive approach — in high technology it is death to miss participating in disruptive technology that will permanently change the state of the value-chain. When Intel was challenged with RISC technology, it offered its own i860 and later Alpha even though non-Microsoft operating systems were favored for those platforms. When Microsoft saw the threat of converged Internet-TV, it brought out its own hardware.

Thousands of firms have successful long-term alliances with Intel, or Microsoft, or both. Their successful partners do not feel that either giant owes them anything. Allies recognize that a partnership is built by adding value to each party.

San Juan Island's Pig War

One famous on-again, off-again relationship is that between America and England. After the War of 1812, hundreds of beautiful islands were divided at the 49th parallel between America and then England's Canada. The 49th parallel went down the middle of San Juan Island.

One day, an English pig ventured into an American farmers potato patch, and, you guessed it, pigged-out. The American shot the English pig. Tempers escalated. Troops on both sides gathered. Each nation built a fort at opposite ends of the island. The countries were on the edge of war. It took twelve years of skillful negotiations between British Admirals and American commanders, plus the intervention of Kaiser Wilhelm of Germany to stop the war. Amazingly, there was only one casualty in twelve years – the pig.

Moral: When you are in the middle of competitive giants— don't be a pig.

Do partners Fake Orgasms?

Your engineers just created the world's greatest electronic mousetrap. They assure you that the world will beat a path to your door.

This mousetrap has high-bandwidth wireless communication, global satellite positioning, multi-processing, and artificial intelligence. In one study, it even caught a mouse. Random Research predicts a market of $10 billion in 5 years. To impress the venture capitalists (VCs), you are forecasting only owning 55% of the market.

Before the VCs will invest $10 million, they tell you to get some major strategic partners: "You need to scale the company." They will not let you use their money to hire 100 sales people. A VC tells you to form a major alliance with corporation employing over 1,000 sales people.

So you go to a leader in your industry and give them your PowerPoint presentation about how you will get rich together. You hint that a major VC is ready to invest and you might let this industry leader in on the deal. They suspect that you are crazy. Just to hedge their bets, three months later, they finally tell you that they will form a strategic alliance.

What have they got to lose? If you do have a breakthrough product, then they partnered with you before the competition did. If you do not, they did not give you any money or promise anything. You have an announcement. You invite the press. If you pay your marketing communications firm over $10,000 per month, a few members of the press actually show-up. More likely, you send a press release to everyone with an email address.

That press release is as far as 95% of all strategic alliances ever go. Next week, your beautiful partner will be sleeping with someone else. The press release is only the first step. The following approach is needed.

How to Make a Strategic Alliance Succeed

✓ **All the steps we discussed in the channel management chapter must be carefully executed to succeed:**

> ✓ Strategy
> ✓ Coverage
> ✓ Mindshare
> ✓ Marketing

- ✓ **Partner Relationship Management**
- ✓ **Teaming**
- ✓ **Money**

Strategy starts with goals that are important to each party. In our example of the start-up with the world's greatest electronic mousetrap, their goals are to secure a first-reference customer and secure $10 million of investment. The goal of their large partner could be to achieve competitive advantage and equity ownership in the startup. The two firms should create a plan to achieve their goals.

Mindshare is just as important with alliances as it is with resellers. A great meeting between CEOs does not mean that the people in the middle know about your alliance, your products, and your services. You must show the "troops" how the alliance will help them with some of their customers.

Alliances are built one person at a time. Good alliances often start by bringing the partner into one customer. When your teamwork brings success to all, the word will spread.

A make-or-break point is when you secure your first order with one of their customers. 110% effort is needed to meet all the customer's needs. Problems must be addressed candidly. People should be kept informed of how the problem is being resolved. People expect things to go wrong with new products and new relationships. They also expect you to fix all problems.

When the customer has implemented your new product, give lots of credit to your alliance partner. Make their people look like heroes. Spread the word about how everyone achieved their goals, such as your partner keeping their competitor out of the account. Build alliances one customer at a time.

After a visible win, you are ready to implement broader mindshare programs such as training, presentations at each other's meetings, and "beer busts." You are ready to formalize the teaming. Co-marketing can be expanded.

A major step in making an alliance successful is to target co-marketing on one specific market segment. Your sales people need to meet the alliance sales people who handle a targeted market segment and key customers. Trust must be built carefully over time. People must be educated.

The right alliance partnerships create better solutions for customers. Keep building them until everyone reaches their first goals and makes money. Teaming takes time, patience, problem resolution and trust building. Strategic alliances are a key to creating value for customers.

Strategic alliances require patience. Microsoft approached much larger Intel about an alliance over 20 years ago. It took months to even get Intel to look at some "kids" in Washington with a software start-up. The alliance required meetings, training, collaboration, trust building, and success with a mutual customer — IBM. The IBM PC sold millions. The strategic alliance has grown for over 20 years despite conflicts and problems. This alliance has created hundreds of billions of wealth for the shareholders of both firms. Alliances can have incredible payoffs.

Summary

Strategic alliances work when complementary firms work together in delivering customer solutions. An alliance is stable and successful when it forms a compelling solution platform for a market segment.

It is also important to remember that when you are in the middle of competing giants — don't be a pig.

You have the advantage that many of your competitors do not have — a solid channel strategy. They do not extend the strategy to strategic alliances, and they do not effectively manage channels and alliances. You can extend your advantage by focusing different partners on different product lines at different points of the product life cycle. This is detailed in the next chapter.

Executive Action

➤ Have someone accountable for the success of strategic alliances.

➤ Understand the total solution needs of your top customers.

➤ Assemble a team of channel partners and strategic alliances to meet those needs.

➤ Plan a co-marketing, brand-building campaign with alliance partners in a market segment where your risks are minimal if the alliance collapses.

Sales Action

➤ Assemble a team of channel partners and strategic alliances to meet the solution needs of each customer.

➤ "Jump start" an alliance by bringing the partner into one opportunity.

➤ Build trust carefully. Start by sharing information and sales strategy about a customer where your risks are minimal if you lose the customer.

➤ Plan to co-market a program and customer event with your partners and alliances.

7

Product Life Cycle Partner Strategy

Product launches come in four flavors. Each favors a different type of channel partner:

Disruptive — Direct Sales + Alliances
Customer Community Leader — Customer Intimate
Market Dominance — Cost + Creative
Brand Extension — All of the above

Disruptive technology is breakthrough innovation that threatens a market's status quo. If the disruptive technology is widely adapted, the market leader is usually replaced, and the value-chain from suppliers to final customer is fundamentally changed.

To succeed, disruptive product introductions require visionary alliance partners to endorse new technology. We want them to help our technology become a platform for other products and solutions. We need direct sales specialists to launch, and then disseminate the word about our early products. A second stage is "niche leadership" where we need partners who can create a complete solution for customers. Customer intimate partners form a whole product. A third stage is market dominance where cost leader partners, including two-tiered global distribution, are necessary to support the hypergrowth of a product that achieves broad market dominance. A final stage is where a market leader can achieve years of added profits from a product with a winning combination of partners.

If you build a better mousetrap and then wait for the world to come to you, be prepared for a very long wait. Best-selling products start with innovation that is carefully nurtured to market. The path is never a straight line. It is full of surprise and change of direction.

Alexander Graham Bell spent years in a seemingly futile struggle to invent the telephone. His father-in-law constantly encouraged Bell to focus on something more practical that would pay the bills. Bell was encouraged to work instead on a better telegraph, because the entire 260,000-mile infrastructure was in place. When Bell did invent the telephone, no one would buy one. What good was a telephone with no one to call?

Bell was trying to disrupt the highly successful telegraph industry. Innovators are always discouraged in the beginning. Early technology always has defects, reliability problems, and higher costs than the incumbent leader, lacks infrastructure, and lack customers. It takes courage and the strategy of meeting all needs of one customer community at a time.

The telephone only succeeded when a channel partner came to the rescue. Near Yale University, the New Haven District Telephone Company was formed. In their customer community, they installed telephone lines and an 8-line switchboard. To make it easy to be a customer, they rented the phone with the telephone service. During the first year, they installed 21 telephones and printed the first telephone directory. The first success of the telephone is a classic example of focusing on one customer community with a partner who can help create a complete customer solution.

By progressing from one customer community to the next with service provider platforms, millions of nationwide customers were established. Nine years after inventing the telephone, Bell founded AT&T. Bell invented the telephone. It took millions of people and thousands of corporations to create the complete infrastructure and solutions that made the telephone a billion-customer success.

Disruptive Technology

Discontinuous innovations...begin with the appearance of a new category of product that incorporates breakthrough technology enabling unprecedented benefits. It is immediately proposed as the natural replacement for a whole class of infrastructure, winning early converts and enthusiastic predictions of a new world order. But the market is a conservative institution, and it presses back against the new changes. . . .Indeed, sometimes the innovation is never embraced. . . .But in many other cases there comes a flash point of change when the entire marketplace, under the pressure of continually escalating disequilibria in price/performance, shifts its allegiance from the old architecture to the new.

—**Geoffrey Moore**
Inside the Tornado

Geoffrey Moore and Clayton Christensen are two strategic thinkers who have reshaped how we succeed with products throughout their life cycle.

Clayton Christensen wrote a wonderful book, *The Innovator's Dilemma.* He shows how successful companies become prisoners of past success, and ignore disruptive technology. For example, Xerox created the first "windows" interface for computers. This breakthrough innovation was "road blocked" by the inventor's large company bureaucracy. Visicorp was first to market with "windows" for personal computers. It took a tenacious startup named Microsoft to achieve market share leadership.

Geoffrey Moore wrote several strategy books including *Crossing the Chasm* and *Inside the Tornado.* He details how to successful progress through the Technology Adoption Life Cycle. Dr. Moore jolted our thinking with countless examples that demonstrate his insights: "The winning strategy does not just change as we move from stage to stage, it actually reverses the prior strategy."

Products, services, and business processes can drive industry change. Let us look at how disruptive and sustaining innovation must each be handled differently.

An example of sustaining innovation is a music CD player that delivers improved sound. An example of disruptive innovation is a new way to share music over the Internet. The better CD player can easily be introduced to an established market with existing suppliers and distribution channels. When Napster provided a new way to share music on the Internet, existing supply chains and channels were disrupted. Music industry leaders fought Napster with billion dollar lawsuits to protect their intellectual property (and also to protect their market leadership).

Disruptive technology can create millionaires. Yet, disruptive technology has a high failure rate, as investors in hot IPOs discover.

Most products based on disruptive technology start out looking like failures. The guy who invented the wheel was probably ridiculed. Early adopters found it clunky and quick to fall apart. They went back to proven approaches like dragging things. The woman who discovered herbal medicine was banished from the clan for challenging the power of the witch doctor.

Computers are now incredibly successful. At the time of their invention, IBM only saw a total market potential of seven computers, and focused its attention on tabulating equipment.

Innovation has accelerated. We now deal with more product launches. They occur more frequently. When we handle them well, we can reinforce our valuable brand, grow market share, and gain competitive advantage. When we handle them poorly, we go out of business.

Best Channels for Disruptive Technology

Start with direct sales, then customer intimate partners. Bureaucracies of successful companies often kill innovation that "rocks the boat". Established channel partners, especially cost leaders, also kill breakthrough products, which typically cost more in the beginning, but lack volume markets.

On occasion, you get involved with technology that will change your industry. New value-chains will be formed. The first product launch involving a disruptive technology needs to be carefully nurtured in niche markets — first by your own direct team, then with a handful of customer intimate partners that can create niche solutions.

Channel partners are of two minds: They do not want to pioneer for you, or they get upset when they feel left out. If you are used to giving all products to all channels, you will need to educate your channels. When introducing disruptive innovation, explain that a careful rollout of the new product will take a few product generations to be worthy of the time of broad-based channels.

Disruptive technology product launches entail more risk, but can be more rewarding. Ironically, risk can be higher when you try to launch a breakthrough product with existing channels. Examine the early failures of the electric car. The promise is wonderful - save gas and save the environment. Unfortunately, early models were expensive and only had a range of 50 miles.

Automobile dealers have a lot of channel power. In the United States, by law, car sales must go through dealers in 47 states. Dealers focus on making money this month. They see a strong demand for SUVs. Ask them to spend their sales and marketing effort on an expensive electric vehicle that only goes 50 miles, and they will tell you that you are crazy. Early efforts to sell electric vehicles through established channels failed.

Honda has grown by differentiating itself from the competition with vehicles, which are more fuel-efficient and create less damaging emissions. Honda was early in introducing an electric car. Although it was quiet, clean, and compact, it failed to achieve consumer acceptance because of its limited driving range.

Honda did achieve significant commercial success with its compressed natural gas (CNG) fueled Civic. It appealed to fleets that wanted to improve air quality, such as municipal governments and gas utilities.

From this success, Honda went on to greater success with hybrid electric vehicles with driving ranges in excess of 500 miles, and mileage of better than 60 miles per gallon. These hybrid vehicles used both small conventional gas engines, and electric motors that greatly boosted fuel efficiency.

Now, Honda is first to market with a fuel-cell electric vehicle. First Honda worked with all infrastructure providers in a consortium called the California Fuel Cell Partnership. Then it secured critical zero-emission certifications from California and the EPA. Then it started leasing fleets to organizations that established central hydrogen fueling stations. Honda has learned to carefully expand by first meeting the needs of one customer community, then the next.

Customer Community Leader

Being the market leader requires a strategy of first dominating one niche market segment at a time. It requires being very deliberate in your selection of customer intimate and creative partners who can meet all the needs of customers in these niches.

DaimlerChrysler is taking a different niche market approach with electric vehicles. As the world leader in buses, DaimlerChrysler has expanded into compressed natural gas (CNG) buses. These low-emission vehicles are popular in areas where clean air is important. City buses can return to central CNG fueling stations, unlike long-distance trucks, which want thousands of diesel fueling stations in place. CNG is a transition technology to an even cleaner approach.

DaimlerChrysler is selling fuel cell-powered buses. Fuel cells generate their own electricity. Buses have room for power systems that will take several product generations to shrink in size and weight. Buses can return to centralized hydrogen fueling stations, instead of needing a nation wide network of service stations.

DaimlerChrysler is increasingly winning orders for millions of dollars of fuel-cell buses. DaimlerChrysler is succeeding by being first to market with hydrogen-powered buses. They will then be the market share leader in buses in targeted European cities that strongly support environmental protection. Their first 30 fuel cell buses were sold to 10 such European cities.

Over time, they can expand this success into related markets. DaimlerChrysler can expand to fleet vehicles, which would share the same hydrogen fueling stations used by buses. As the population of fuel cell vehicles grows, hydrogen-fueling stations will also grow. Service centers will grow. Parts distributors will take inventory. Established dealers in niche markets will want to carry the product. These dealers will agree to investments in training, marketing, inventory, and more.

The strategy of succeeding with disruptive technology is detailed in Geoff Moore's insightful book, *Crossing the Chasm*. He talks about progressing from one to many market segments as a "Bowling Alley" approach. Knock down the first pin, and the others will follow. If we were to formalize a possible approach for DaimlerChrysler, it could look like this progression from segments one to ten:

	Germany	Europe	USA	Global
CNG buses	1	2	4	7
Fuel-cell buses	3	5	8	
Fleet specialty	6	9		
Fleet autos	10			

DaimlerChrysler will carefully expand one niche at a time, starting with its world leadership in buses. It will start with direct fleet sales, and slowly involve dealers who can help with sales and service of smaller local fleets, such as local delivery businesses.

Honda has started small with electric vehicles, and expands into different market segments as it establishes leadership in early niches. Both Honda and DaimlerChrysler see the trillion dollar global potential of electric fuel cell vehicles. Both recognize the importance of solving many issues of new technology including new fuel cells, drive trains, electronics, fuel tanks, fueling stations, and service.

In a few years, both will compete in a broadly developed market for fuel cell vehicles, just as they now compete for gas-powered cars. Both will be expanding from positions of strength in well-established market segments. They will have loyal partners and customers that will give them significant advantage over the latecomers.

New and Improved

To the optimist, the glass is half full. To the pessimist, the glass is half empty. To the engineer, the glass is twice as big as it needs to be.

Most product launches involve improvements of established products, rather than disruptive technology. Over time, disruptive technology either becomes established or it disappears. Use improved product offerings to take competitive share, reinforce your brand, and improve existing channel revenue.

Oracle was first to market with a breakthrough approach for managing data — the relational database. Oracle became the market share leader by frequently releasing product improvements. It ported its database software to one operating system after another. Soon it was the only database that could run on all the computers owned by large organizations. Oracle listened to customers. It documented all reported "bugs" in the software. It listened to software developers. It frequently released new versions of the Oracle database that responded to these customer needs.

Once it succeeded at being the market leader, Oracle progressed from only using direct sales, to convincing computer corporations and software firms to OEM its database. The top technology companies were now selling Oracle as part of their solutions. Oracle gained thousands of specialized technical support consultants in this way.

Continuously Improved Products and Services

For technology products and services, strategy is not a straight line; it is a continuous loop. A service is launched. A market segment is won. Improvements are made to delight and keep customers. Enhancements are added as added market segment leadership is achieved. Improvement is a customer-driven unending process. It moves at Internet speed.

A current and growing trend is subscription services. The telephone only succeeded when the telephone product was rented with the telephone service. The Honda fuel-cell automobile is leased with warranty services. Increasingly, software is subscribed as a service rather than sold as a product.

You subscribe to products and services that must be constantly improved. Your favorite magazine is constantly trying to deliver a better product to you. They do not have years to carefully plan and execute a product launch. At best they have a month. The Wall Street Journal became the first publisher to have over one million pay for subscribing to their Internet publication. They improve the product every minute. They also empower customers to customize the look and content of the publication. One person reads the publication on a large screen with a focus on one specific industry. Other people read the Wall Street Journal on their cell phones and hand-held computers.

Like other forward thinking software firms, Oracle is rethinking its business. It is expanding from products to the subscription of continually improved software and services. Some businesses want Internet access to software that Oracle runs on remote servers. Oracle can improve the software daily. Oracle can provide various support services. Oracle can extend this model to a new type of channel partner — the Application Service Provider (ASP).

Subscription services are first offered directly by the software developer, then by value partners such as ASPs. Once market share leadership is achieved, then cost leader partners can deliver the added global capacity necessary for market dominance. For example, Reuters first offers financial information services to large banks, then through other specialty information providers, and finally through thousands of online stockbrokers and publishers.

Oracle is reaching the point where they are adding cost leader partners to reach millions of added businesses. Wells Fargo Bank offers small business subscribers the monthly use of the Oracle database and applications for small businesses. Behind the scenes, it is really Oracle who is running the software and providing support. Next, we could see major telephone companies offering database usage, just like they offer dial tone.

Market Dominance with Cost Leader Partners

When you expand sales channels you do not automatically increase sales. If your new channels are successful, you have more "feet on the street" selling for you. If you handle the delicate change improperly, you lose the loyalty of existing channel members and lower your total sales. Risk is moderate if you expand carefully, and focus on improved extensions to existing product families.

Symantec is a highly successful software company. You may use one or more of their Norton software products to protect your computers from viruses, crashes, and problems. They have well-established cost-leader channel partners such as Best Buy, Office Depot, and Amazon. Symantec has major opportunities as more home-based small businesses are established, and as more homes install sophisticated, high speed networks. Symantec can expand its channels to include telephone service providers with added networking expertise. They can grow revenues by introducing improved products through additional partners.

They need to expand carefully, and simultaneously protect their relationships with their existing channel partners. They can do this by training existing partners on new products. They can give them special attention with dedicated teams, custom marketing campaigns and added marketing funds.

Working with strategic allies is another way to expand market share. A strategic alliance typically involves the cooperation of two corporations in their sales and marketing. They normally do not resell each other's products. Instead they work together to meet common goals. For years, Symantec has successfully partnered with Microsoft, rather than compete. The two firms can compare notes on who are the best channel partners for product types. Symantec can leverage Microsoft's brand and enormous marketing budget.

Market Dominance with Creative Leader Partners

Market dominance is often achieved by being inside other products. From health products to automotive parts to computer chips, successes have started by exposing innovation to technical people and visionaries. Then, while working to be the leader in a customer community, firms also get "designed in" to future products being created by other companies. Market dominance is the reward as these independent products ship in volume.

Palm makes an exciting passel of handheld computers. Palm protects its market dominance by being a platform for thousands of handheld software applications, by creating an opportunity to sell millions of plug-in cards, and by being at the heart of many other products. The Palm operating system is found inside Smartphones from Kyocera, Sony Personal Entertainment Handhelds, Symbol Technologies Handheld Wireless Barcode Scanners, Acer Chinese-Language Palm Computers, and hundreds of other electronic devices.

The PalmSource subsidiary of Palm achieved these critical design wins by providing a market leading platform, forming strategic alliances, providing tools to developers, and packaging marketing programs for its OEM and software partners. Palm has provided software tools and developer kits to over 200,000 developers.

Palm established these strategic partnerships to protect its market dominance, reach added millions of customers in all corners of the earth, and create added streams of income. Palm also established these partnerships so that it could extend its brand.

Brand Extension

Normal people . . .believe that if it ain't broke, don't fix it. Engineers believe that if it ain't broke, it doesn't have enough features yet."

— Scott Adams
The Dilbert Principle

Brand extensions accelerate revenue rockets. Brand extensions normally involve existing sales channels. This is often successful when products are well-established with a wide audience.

In 1928, Walt Disney created Mickey Mouse. In the beginning, there was one distribution channel – movie theaters. By 1932, Mickey and Minnie's faces were on toys and clothes. There was the Mickey Mouse Book, and internationally syndicated comic strips. By year's end, 80 major U.S. corporations were selling The Walt Disney Company merchandise. Walt Disney is a Revenue Rocket Hall of Fame leader for his brilliance in extending the brand, and selling the products through an array of publishing and product distribution channels. Where others saw a Great Depression, Walt Disney envisioned endless opportunities to make people happy.

The Walt Disney Company has done an amazing job of extending its brand, and giving a famous mouse a very long life. Mickey Mouse is an example of how creative developers, marketers, and channel managers can make their companies billions by extending the life of a product.

Any parent with young children will tell you that the presence of Mickey Mouse continues to extend into a family of theater experiences, cable TV premium services, video tapes, DVDs, printed books, audio books, combination audio-print bundles, interactive CD-ROMs, stuffed animals, and theme parks. That mouse touches the far ends of this earth.

The Walt Disney Company creates sales leverage with an effective mix of direct sales, creative, customer intimate, and cost leader partners. It forms alliances to reach new countries. It sells through channels from specialized children's learning centers to mass merchandisers.

Use specialized partners to adopt your market leading products to new market segments. These are creative and customer intimate partners with segment expertise. Also use brand extension product launches to generate new excitement with your cost leader partners. Let customers buy through their preferred channel.

Partner Focus

There are a number of ways to achieve the focus of desired partners at appropriate stages of the lifecycle. First, only authorize partners when a product is ready for them. Honda's global dealers are not ready for a fuel cell car. There needs to be testing, improvements, safety testing, local government approval, and careful rollout in markets that have the infrastructure over a period of years. In partner agreements, it is necessary to have the ability to authorize sales by products and product lines. You do not need to authorize all partners for all products.

Customer community leadership precedes broad market dominance. Your partner business plans can be incorporated into your partner agreement. Market segments can be specified. You can involve partners in market segment programs based on segments specified in business plans. Leading websites allow potential customers to search for partners based on applications, products, geography, and sophisticated segmentation. Ask your partners to select only their top categories before including them in these search engines. Do not let them check every box on the form.

Specialized certification training can be offered. Partners in the area of specialty will meet the prerequisites and enroll. This represents an investment of valuable sales and technical employee time. Most partners will not participate. Market segmented channel programs can require special certification in order to participate. By asking partners to invest, self-selection naturally occurs.

A continual challenge for channel managers is the involvement of cost leader channels. Because of size and efficiency, they often under price the very customer intimate partners who made the product successful in the first place. Yet, without your cost leaders global market dominance will not occur. Your competition will walk away with the market.

There are many ways to keep your specialized and customer intimate partners happy. One is to make your product line a platform for their highly profitable services. Keep them focused on early customer community and later brand extension programs where the partners add significant value and achieve significant profits.

Consider creating separate brands for cost leader partners. Sony is very selective in partners that are authorized to sell its complex broadcast equipment. At the same time, the Sony Walkman product line is available from many competing cost leaders around the globe. Further, to reach the aggressive price points demanded in many regions of the globe, Sony offers consumer entertainment products without the Sony brand name.

When successful products reach the brand extension stage, specific integrated marketing campaigns can be created by market segment. Authorize partners to select one, and only one, segment where they can use their MDF to participate in the campaign. Generate leads, and electronically distribute them by partner self-selected market segments.

Summary

Disruptive technology achieves initial success when a dedicated direct team nurtures it. The team is focused on one leader in a specific market segment. The team needs to understand and solve all the needs of one customer at a time.

New product market leadership is achieved by dominating one segment at a time. Strategic allies and value partners help create complete solutions. The best partners have a strong presence in the targeted market. These partners make their money from their own services. Engage partners that own the segments, add value and have major opportunities with their services. These may not be your traditional channels.

Most product launches involve improvements to an existing product. Use your existing channels to grow your market leadership. Make them fully ready for announcement day by training them in advance. Arm them with marketing materials. Use the new product as a way to grow channel "mindshare."

Use brand extension strategies to give added years of success to your best product lines. Once again, segment the market. Help partners with marketing programs focused on specific segments to grow your share in each segment.

Selectively involving partners at different phases of the product lifecycle can save millions over old-fashion approaches of shipping expensive marketing kits and sample products to all partners at all times. At the right times, partners can accomplish more, for less money, than direct sales teams. The next chapter details how to get more revenue, while lowering total sales and marketing costs.

Executive Action

➢ Have an internally published innovation plan.

➢ Have an externally published statement of direction.

➢ Use disruptive product offerings to leap frog the competition and create new markets. Only involve channel partners that offer significant value in the targeted market segment.

➢ Use sustaining innovation to take competitive share, reinforce your brand, and improve existing channel revenue.

Sales Action

➢ Ensure that your top channel partners are fully prepared to answer questions and take orders the day of a new product announcement.

➢ Use product launches as an opportunity to develop "mindshare" with your customers and channel partners.

➢ For disruptive products start with the customer intimate leaders in one target segment.

➢ Sell services that ensure that your customers are always benefiting from the latest products and getting 24/7 support.

8

Big Results with a Tight Budget

Make it easy for partners to spend their money promoting your products.

Focus On Channels

When budgets are tight, most corporations should increase the emphasis on channels, and lower the cost of direct sales. Direct sales coverage should be limited to the large global accounts that produce a high return on your sales investment.

Direct sales coverage of a major account can easily cost $500,000 in annual payroll. Channel coverage might cost only 10% of that. With direct coverage you need a team of people. Your team could include a sales executive, an inside salesperson, and a system engineer. With the right channel partner you can gain ten people to cover the account, and benefit from the long-term relationship of the channel partner with the account, and provide the customer with partner, value-added solutions.

Direct sales coverage is important with strategic global customers. A direct account manager can better manage a large global account than can a local channel partner. Use direct teams to cover your most important global accounts. Most companies should not cover geographies with direct sales; they should use channels for broader coverage.

Less is More

The 80/20 rule applies to channel sales. Invest in training, mindshare, and marketing programs with your best partners. Focus on the top 20% of partners in order to accelerate revenue and lower sales cost.

Over time, a corporation may find that it has grown to have 5,000 resellers. It may discover that 1,000 resellers generate at least 80% of the revenue. These top resellers are likely to be loyal, better trained, demand creators, and be profitable. It is tempting to leave the other 4,000 alone. Maybe they will sell something. What would you do with these 4,000? If you terminate them, you worry about legal problems. You worry that they will go to the competition. You worry that you will not make revenue goals.

Your worst partners often bid down the "street price," removing incentive for your value-added partners to develop new business. *Too many resellers lower revenue.*

If you keep all 5,000, you may be legally obligated to offer expensive training and marketing programs to all partners. Having fewer partners lowers these costs. You can give more attention to your best partners when you are not wasting time trying to fix your worst ones. If you terminate the worst 10% of your partners every six months, your channel profits will increase. Terminating and recruiting are ongoing parts of channel management.

Good agreements with channel partners make it easy to weed out the worst. Contracts include provisions for termination when training certification requirements are not met. Sales reporting compliance is required. It is essential to have the right to terminate without cause.

Smart Recruiting

Many firms spend too much money on recruiting channel partners. The "less is more" approach may show that you do not need to spend a fortune in recruiting new partners. A modest investment in training and marketing with existing partners will often generate business faster than investing in new partners.

Why recruit an unknown reseller with 500 salespeople, when only 100 of the 1,000 salespeople of an existing reseller are promoting your product?

Expensive recruiting campaigns are often counter-productive. A potential partner should be targeted exclusively. They want to feel special. A personal letter and an executive one-to-one meeting are the best ways to approach the best potential partners.

Large strategic allies can open the doors to their partners, if they trust you and feel that they add value. When Veritas was developing channels, it went to the channel managers of major computer companies and asked about their best channel partners. Veritas targeted the best, with the help of strategic allies. No mass marketing was needed to build this $2 billion enterprise software giant.

Strategic Allies

Strategic allies can stretch your sales budget in countless ways. Identify your ten best strategic allies. Meet with them to explore how you can better coordinate sales and marketing. You will accelerate revenues, build channel loyalty, and lower your sales cost.

Veritas' use of allies for recruiting is a good example. Not only can you work with allies in recruiting partners, you can work with them in recruiting customers. For example, major corporations are paranoid about losing priceless information. These customers will invest millions in sophisticated storage systems to manage information. Sun Microsystems and Veritas create co-marketing to generate interest. They save millions by sharing the costs for advertising, direct marketing, trade shows, and events.

Adding more allies can lower costs even further. By including Cisco, a manufacturer of sophisticated switches, as an ally, Sun and Veritas can lower sales costs. Sales are increased. Three sales forces can coordinate their efforts and stretch sales coverage. Customers can be convinced faster. Sun says Veritas and Cisco are great. Veritas tells the customer that Sun and Cisco are great. You get the idea. So does the customer.

This co-marketing can be extended to shared channel partners. Co-marketing can be packaged for common channel partners. Special promotions can be created. Bundles of complementary products can be promoted by one of the allies, by all, or by a distributor in the middle.

Disappearing Discounts

✓ **Focus on the end-customer to avoid destroying profits at the end of a quarter.**

Elizabeth Budzynska, Vice President of Global Sales at Aethra, complained about another firm earlier in her career: "We trained our distributors to buy from us on the last hour of the last day of a quarter." The company was determined to make aggressive quarterly goals. Distributors learned to play "chicken" each quarter, and win. Deep discounts simply lowered "street prices." Deep discounts meant that it took 20% more products to achieve the same revenue.

In order to break the cycle of these "last hour" negotiations, focus on co-marketing and team selling with partners. Focus on creating more sales with the final customers. Help them create strong end-user demand at the start of the quarter. If they have no inventory, they will need to order early or lose business to their competition. Using a deep discount to stuff the channel shelves, does not add revenue. It simply destroys the next quarter. We will look at more solutions in the next chapter.

Pre-Package Marketing

This real-life marketing challenge could only occur in California. Bob Eubank, then president of Ocean Imports, wanted to sell health food for tropical fish. Bob asked if I could create the advertising campaign with a total ad budget of only $1,000 per month. I could not resist this challenge. First, we actively debated about the targeted customer community. We focused on the demographics of serious tropical fish hobbyist, often with advanced university degrees, and a willingness to pay premium *prices for specialized fish food. A high-end tropical fish journal was selected for low-cost half-page ads.*

With a theme of keeping the fish alive longer, Bob and I brainstormed over 50 ad headlines. We were tempted to use humor, such as a police line-up of house servants, a butler holding a dead goldfish, and the headline "Who killed Goldie?" We were tempted by a line of fish sitting at an ice cream counter, with the headline "21 Flavors." We settled on a long headline complete with a product benefit statement and the product name. After running the ad for 30 days, sales had tripled. In four months, sales had increased 600%. To get big results with a tight budget, focus on a customer community with a compelling underserved need. Often, it is better to target the decision-maker. We wisely decided not to target the ultimate consumers of the food, because they had no money, they could not read, and they preferred to just swim around while blowing bubbles.

Get your channel partners to spend their money promoting your products. The best firms target market segments with high growth potential. These firms package channel partner campaigns aimed at these segments.

A storage company might target firms with large libraries of high-resolution images and streaming video. They might refine the segment to ten thousand mid-sized advertising and communication firms. Then they would provide channel partners with the right mailers, brochures, advertisement copies, telemarketing scripts, and PowerPoint presentations.

To get even more from a tight budget, the storage company could distribute all this in digital form to their partners. They could make it even easier for the partner to create their own custom ads, brochures, and promotions. They could provide them with a database of leads, telemarketing and print-on-demand firms that could execute the campaign for a partner with a push of the button.

Rather than spending your money to create demand, encourage your partners to spend their money. Many have accumulated marketing development funds (MDF), which could be used to pay for end-user demand creation.

Just in Time for Everything

Use the Internet to be more closely linked with your channel partners. Be more closely linked than any of your competitors.

We have seen that there was a magical thinking about the Internet, including the belief that it would eliminate channels. Instead, you can make your channel relationships much more efficient with the Internet and e-business applications.

Use Partner Relationship Management (PRM) to manage the implementation of pre-packaged marketing. PRM allows you to automatically distribute marketing content to your channels, implement marketing campaigns and track the results.

Everything we have discussed about channel marketing and sales should be supported with a private website for your partners. You want to arm your partners with all the latest sales and marketing tools for their one-touch implementation. This approach can save millions of dollars of printing and express delivery of everything from brochures to reference manuals.

When you have a great partner website, do not stop there. Update your partner's websites so that your latest information is instantly available to their customers.

Just-in-time efficiencies are maximized when investments are made in extranets that link you with partners. PRM automates much of demand creation, order processing, support, and sales effectiveness.

Everyone wants just-in-time products, services, and information. Put systems in place for rapid response to save money over older approaches of excess inventory everywhere, printing, and shipping everything. Electronically arm channel sales and marketing with the latest tools, pricing, and product information.

Empowered Customer and Partner Support

Delighted customers are lifetime customers. Rather than hiring another thousand people to support your customers, empower your customers to help themselves. Also, give your partners the best training and tools to support customers.

Cisco is the world's most successful maker of network switches. Chances are that your phone calls and computer connections go through their switches. When a network switch has a problem, people get very upset, very fast.

Cisco allows customers to go to a website where libraries of updated help manuals are available. If the customer has a support contract, they can talk to a live person, download software patches, or join collaborative Internet discussions with network engineers. A customer can even take online courses about networks and problem resolution.

Eighty percent of Cisco's global business is through channel partners. Partners usually offer customers a mix of Cisco support services and the partners' own services. Partners are required to put network engineers through extensive Cisco training and to be certified. If a Cisco channel partner does not have properly certified engineers, it can be terminated. Partners have password-protected websites with extensive tools to configure systems, diagnose problems and download software fixes.

Collaboration is common between network engineers. The result is that 70% of the time, customers resolve their own problems without talking to a Cisco person. This saves Cisco over $250 million in annual support costs. Customers and partners are happy. Networks keep running.

"Webinars" and E-learning

Another way to save money is to replace some customer events with Web-based seminars ("Webinars"). Replace traditional classroom learning with e-learning.

Marketing managers used to spend at least $10,000 per customer seminar to get potential buyers into expensive hotel ballrooms. As customers started working on Internet time, marketing people have become more desperate to get seats filled. Now customers can view presentations, hear presenters and interact through their Web browser. You can also reach partners and customers around the world, at the same time. This is especially valuable when launching a new product or service.

The Cisco Partner E-Learning Connection includes fee-based courses for network engineers, and free product updates. Global partners get up-to-the minute learning at their convenience. Cisco saves tens of millions. Learners register, and then track their learning progress. Several learning formats include video on-demand programs, virtual hands-on labs, online mentors, testing, and reference libraries.

Ninety percent of all Cisco partners use the E-Learning Connection. Over 200,000 people around the globe are kept up-to-date in a cost effective approach.

Clone Successes

Individual channel partners often do something brilliant. When this happens, they encourage similar partners in other geographies to do the same.

A partner may promote a new application for your product. Sales accelerate. Clone it. Another partner may create new integrated marketing of newspaper ads, radio spots, direct marketing, and telemarketing. The campaign works, and sales increase. Teach other partners to do the same.

You may have ten smart channel sales and marketing people at your headquarters. They create some good ideas, but have trouble testing the ideas with end-customers. They may also have their internal bureaucracy to overcome. Your global channel partners may have 10,000 employees creating ideas. They constantly test these ideas in various market segments. Stay close to your partners; you will learn a great deal. See what works and clone it.

Summary

Channel partners can grow revenue for corporations, and lower sales costs. Partners already have major investments in trained people, processes, and customer service. They can add complementary products for less money than the brand provider would need to spend on added payroll. Reevaluate the focus of specific partners to better serve specific market segments.

The key to success is to make it easy for partners to spend their money promoting your products. Create extensive marketing campaigns that partners can access through your private partner website. Provide partners with training and knowledge transfer, which empowers their success. Observe what works with one partner, and clone that success with others.

It is important to do the right things with partners. It is equally important to avoid the critical mistakes detailed in the next chapter.

Executive Action

➤ Invest 80% of your resources in the 20% of your channels most committed to your products and services.

➤ Assign strategic global accounts, not general territories, to direct sales teams.

➤ Meet with your top 10 channel partners and strategic allies. Commit to specific co-marketing and co-sales.

Sales Action

➤ Invest 80% of your resources in the 20% of your channels most committed to your products and services.

➤ Always encourage partners to have more sales and technical people knowledgeable about your products and services. Keep a database of trained partner people.

➤ Meet with your top 10 channel partners. Plan different marketing campaigns with each that use MDF.

➤ Partners and customers should be sold training and support programs that empower them to resolve their own problems 24/7.

➤ Clone successes.

9

Ten Mistakes to Avoid With Partners

1. **Confusing Partners with Final Customers**
2. **Confusing Press Releases with Partners**
3. **Stuffing the Channels**
4. **Expecting Distributors to give you an Instant Channel**
5. **Believing that More Resellers = More Revenue**
6. **Taking Partners for Granted**
7. **Failing to Train**
8. **Failing to Arm Partners for Battle**
9. **Ignoring Demand Creation**
10. **Going Directly to Jail**

It took me seventeen years to get 3,000 hits in baseball. I did it in one afternoon on the golf course.

— Hank Aaron

TO AVOID:

Confusing Partners with Final Customers

You can be the market leader, if you never confuse an order with a customer. The person, or business, which pays for your products, is of ultimate importance. Your continued success depends upon keeping customers happy. You build lifetime customer relationships with final customers.

You have created a value-chain of partners to grow your business with these final customers. Your partners should ensure customer satisfaction. Your value-chain should offer the fast response and service that makes these customers want to increase their business with you, and spread the word to their friends.

Many companies become lazy. They ship products to a distributor, and then consider the sale complete. Some corporations do not even know the names of their final customers. These companies are vulnerable to competitors who develop deep knowledge about customers. Smart competition will create a value-chain that offers better solutions and support.

Confusing Press Releases with Partners

Create long-term strategic allies. Do not commit "serial polygamy." Have a planning session with each of your partners. The result will be agreed upon goals, plans of action, and commitments from you and them. Then, execute the plan.

Strategic Technologies is a regional solution integrator for Sun Microsystems, HP, and other leading product companies. With Sun, the relationship started with a strategic plan.

The plan included goals, financial projections, target markets in North Carolina, marketing campaigns, service programs, hiring, and training plans. Both Strategic Technology and Sun agreed to action items with people's names, deadlines and budget commitments. Both executed successfully. Strategic Technologies CEO, Mike Shook, built his profitable business from ground zero to over $100 million in less than ten years. Each time he forms a partnership, he looks past the press release that announces the partnership. His team creates a strategic plan and makes it happen.

Stuffing the channels

Your goal should be to advance your career and make more money by doing the right thing for everyone. Your goal should not be to make this quarter's numbers in a way that will get you fired next quarter. There is a better way to simultaneously make the quarter and build long-term business.

The phrase *stuffing the channels* refers to convincing distributors and resellers to take large inventory positions. These resellers will insist on a large discount, extended credit, unlimited returns, or all of these before they will take your inventory.

In the last chapter, we discussed distributors who learned that they could "play chicken" with their suppliers, and stretch their 40% discount to 60%

discounts at the end of a quarter. Not only was revenue lost in the added discount, but partnerships were also destroyed. The channel partners who created end-customer demand, and offered the best service, were not getting as big of a discount as their low-cost competitors.

The next quarter, the low-cost players offer deep discounts to get business created by the value-leaders. Then, value leaders would get fed-up and take their business to a competitive manufacturer. A vicious cycle was created where everyone loses: the manufacturer's profit margins shrink, channel managers must sell more units at deep discounts to achieve the same revenue numbers, channel partners make no added money because the final customer gets a big discount, the final customer buys from a distributor who cannot afford to install and support the systems.

How do you break this cycle? First, help your top channel partners offer highly profitable services based on your products. Second, implement demand creation programs early in the quarter that your partners can use to sell-out their entire inventory. Use Partner Relationship Management (PRM) to implement the demand creation, and track channel sales. Third, be courageous with your channel integrity. Give all partners who are at the same tier, the same discount. Fourth, when you must get aggressive to make your quarterly numbers, package special promotions that are consistent across all channels. Fifth, be prepared for channel partners who love to negotiate. Distributors and other cost leaders are better at this than anyone else. They will tell you that they must get an added 10% to save your 50-unit order from going to your competitor. Handle this by giving the final customer the 10% discount regardless of which channel partner they use, only if they accept delivery by the end of the quarter. Final point: do not stuff the channel.

Expecting Distributors to give you an Instant Channel

Distributors are excellent at order processing, logistics, and credit lines for resellers. They are rarely effective with partner recruiting and marketing. That is your job. A few will do a good job of recruiting and marketing if you give them specific guidelines, daily direction, and enough money.

When deciding whether to go to two-tiered distribution, evaluate whether your cost savings in outsourcing inventory management, sales, support, and other costs justify the added discount. Do not be captivated by the distributors size or number of resellers. Expect to drive end-user demand and channel sales.

This could happen to you. A small software firm felt that their road to riches would be in signing a major distributor. They did get a major distributor to agree to carry their products. They advanced the distributor upfront marketing funds, and dropped their discount from the 30% that they gave to other resellers, to 45% to the billion-dollar giant distributor. They shipped a thousand copies of their software in expensive packages that included a printed manual and software on CDs. They invoiced the distributor for $250,000, and then waited for the flood of orders.

The flood never came. Not even a trickle. They released an updated version of the software. Their invoice to the distributor was uncollected after 90 days. They pressed the distributor to pay them. Finally, the distributor returned the entire inventory, claiming it was obsolete. They never received a nickel.

Believing that More Resellers = More Revenue

If you add too many resellers, their profit margins will disappear and so will your revenue. Focus on maximizing profits with the right number of channel partners.

The confusion starts by thinking that every business that is authorized to sell your products is doing something to promote your product. When you have hundreds of resellers, many will do nothing more than take an order. You need partners who are actively marketing and selling your product, then giving customers effective support. Partners can only afford to market your products, if they have adequate profit margin. Thus, too many resellers result in disappearing margins and sales.

Segment your market into a matrix of product and market segments, as we detailed in the channel strategy chapter. For each segment, determine the number of partners that will maximize your sales minus the costs. Some partners will help in many of these segments. This bottoms-up approach will lead you to the optimal number of partners.

Taking Partners for Granted

Your channel partners have a choice. They can devote their time to selling for you, or for other companies. Treat them like a partner. Help channel partners to build their business.

In 1999, Ford Motor made Jacques Nasser CEO. Two years later he was gone. Mr. Nasser was committed to reinventing Ford. He tried to tell Ford dealers what to do. Sales and marketing initiatives were created that bypassed the customer. The problem is that the auto dealers sell the vast majority of Ford vehicles.

William Clay Ford Jr. is now running Ford. He is committed to having a dialogue with the dealers. He listens. The dealers have deep insights into what is going on in the market. They often sell competitive brands. They are closest to the customer. Dealers make increasing money from customer services. They want help in building lifetime customer relationships with creative service programs, leasing, and upgrading customers to new models.

You can grow channel partner mindshare by listening. You can create dialogue through one-to-one discussions, partner advisory councils, surveys, and collaboration on the Internet. The idea is to continually understand their issues and help partners grow their business.

Failing to Train

✓ **People sell and support what they know.**

One key to Microsoft's success is the investment that they make in training their channel partners. Microsoft has a University for its partners. In addition, Microsoft has global training partners who teach hundreds of courses for resellers and customers. Microsoft invests heavily in e-learning, and hundreds of Web-based courses are also available.

In preparing to launch WindowsXP, Microsoft trained thousands of partners. Microsoft offered technical training, sales training, and application training. It offered the training in many forms, including instructor delivered and Web-based. Microsoft went beyond training about the product's features. It taught partners how to improve the sales of their profitable services in enterprise network management, application implementation, wireless solutions, and specific industry solutions.

Partners were invited to attend the event where Bill Gates announced the product. If they could not be there in person, they could see and hear Bill on the Internet. Live people were available over the phone and Internet to answer partner questions. The day of the big product launch, channel partners were prepared, knowledgeable, and taking orders. A key to Microsoft's multi-billion dollar success is its investment in training its partners.

Failing to Arm Partners for Battle

Your partners typically sell for hundreds of firms. Give them better sales and marketing tools than anyone else and you win. Fail to give them tools and you lose.

Your partners also need pre-packaged and integrated marketing that is focused on your products and services. They want up-to-the-minute digital files for them to use in placing advertising. They want to modify the advertisements and include their own logo. They want video and audio files for TV and radio advertising. Partners want to be given brochures and mailers, or be able to easily buy them with marketing development funds (MDF).

Partners want kits for dealing with the press. They want a roadmap to gain more publicity. If you have a hot company, they want to be associated with you.

Companies want you to update their websites automatically, or run your portion of their website for them. Use a partner website and call center to give partner sales people fast answers to the questions that customers will give them. If your products are complex, provide partners with proposal libraries. For complex products, provide technical configuration tools.

Partner websites and Compact Discs are excellent ways to give partners the marketing tools and technical documentation that they need. Do a better job than your competition and you will grow your business. Arm partners to win the battle for profitable business.

Ignoring Demand Creation

Do not ignore helping your channels create customer demand. Your company can create end-customer demand for your products. Your channel partners can also create demand for your products. You want to make both happen. Develop co-marketing that creates leverage, growth, and the building of a great brand.

Your brand is the way that your customers experience your product. Most customers form their opinions about your brand through their dealings with your partners. You want to build a great brand by developing delighted customers who buy your products repeatedly.

Use integrated marketing communication to create customer demand. In combination, advertise, form allies, form channels, manage public relations, create sales promotions, direct markets, and market on the Internet.

Involve your channel advisory council in creating and reviewing the marketing communication plans and message. Involve the marketing executives of your best channel partners. Plan from the beginning to have channel marketing activities integrated with your own. When you launch a new product, or new marketing campaign, give your channels all the marketing tools in advance so that their activities are coordinated with yours.

Partner relationship management (PRM) is an excellent platform to manage the content distribution, management and analysis of marketing campaigns. Channel salespeople want leads. PRM can be an excellent way to automate the distribution of leads to the best partner. PRM can also let you track the results.

Channel salespeople want to work with your sales team. They want your sales and technical people to join them on key sales calls. Channel marketing people want to work with your marketing people.

Going Directly to Jail

Every country has specific laws about channels of distribution. You want to obey these laws.

In the United States, you need to be concerned about anti-trust, collusion, franchise laws, and unfair business practices. States may have specific laws. For example, most U.S. states insist that cars must be purchased from a local dealer. You cannot tell a reseller at what price to sell. You must treat all partners in a class the same way.

When you are managing channels, you need to educate everyone in your company about how to deal with channel partners. Your firm's direct sales people, for example, may tell a partner the price that they should quote. They may say: "Stay out of my account." This could put your company in a lawsuit, or land someone in jail.

Publish your policies on your internal Internet site, and partner site. Educate. Encourage team building between direct sales and partners. Be consistent in managing your channel programs.

Summary

Success starts with treating partners like partners. They do not want to be loaded with inventory, and then left to fend for themselves. They will carry the load if you help them down the right highway. Start them with their training, marketing programs, and working with them as a team. With momentum, expect them to initiate and lead growth.

At this point in the book, you have absorbed the new strategies that create partner excellence. You have examined how to get big results, and avoid critical mistakes.

The idea of partnership implies people working together. In the next section, you will see how great companies deploy sales teams to work with the largest customers. You will see how direct sales works in partnership with distribution channels whenever it is in their best interest financially, and to achieve customer satisfaction. The future of sales will be founded on partner excellence, real-time information, and superior communication. See to it that you create sales leverage in constructing your very own Revenue Rocket.

Executive Action

- ➢ Make everyone "customer-centric" and "partner-centric" through executive leadership and training

- ➢ Integrate corporate and channel marketing.

- ➢ Achieve quarterly financial goals through a process of promotions and channel-neutral discounts to final customers. Do not stuff the channels.

- ➢ Implement Partner Relationship Management (PRM) to automate marketing content management, sales leads, sales tracking, MDF management

- ➢ If you already have PRM, integrate it with your back-end databases and enterprise applications.

Sales Action

> ➢ Start each quarter with a specific plan and forecast to achieve 300% of quarter. Do not show the plan to management, or they will increase your goal. Execute the plan, and you will never need to stuff your channels.

> ➢ Involve top partner marketing executives in the design of new marketing campaigns.

> ➢ Thoroughly learn your company's CRM and PRM. Use them to distribute leads, implement marketing, and track results.

Part Three

Sales Leverage

10

Lifetime Customers and Lightspeed Response

> **20% of customers = 80% of profits. Create lifetime customers with lightspeed response.**

✓ **Customers pay our bills. They sponsor our careers.**

Meeting their needs profitably is our mission. With our best customers, the relationship is like a partnership. We are seen as part of their organization.

There are important dimensions to customer relationships including lightspeed response, sales teams, and channel partners. Use these to build lasting customer relationships. The ultimate customer of our products and services, the end-customer, evaluates us based on their experiences with our channel partners. If the end-customer loves the delivered solution, of which we are a part, then the customer loves us. If they dislike partner solutions or support, they dislike us. Our brands are shaped by our value-chain. We are what the customer experiences.

Lifetime Customers

Everyday you are a customer. You know what it is like to be treated well. You love it when a company remembers you, and your preferences, then delivers more than you expected. A customer intimate specialty store gets you a beautiful, one-of-a-kind item that you asked about on your last visit. An operationally efficient delivery service absolutely, positively gets the right documents to you on time, every time. Your creative leader has invented a combination cell phone and palm computer that takes perfect dictation.

Successful firms are passionate about their customers. It really shows when you deal with their sales and support people. In this time of unparalleled change, customer intimate leaders thrive while uncaring confused companies fail to survive. The recent implosion of dot-com companies was full of get-rich quick schemes. Many of the firms were not passionate about their customers. Many did not even know their customers.

Customer intimate leaders often have teams onsite at major customers' offices. Team members may have their own desk at the customers' offices. They may wear the same identification badge that is worn by customer employees. In a call center, a supplier phone number may be imbedded in the phone system of the customer. Best customers may see team members as virtual employees.

Virtual Teams

Smart corporations focus on what they do best. They outsource the rest. These top corporations involve channel partners to drive most sales. The best corporations are virtual corporations. A virtual corporation is one where everyone acts like they work for the same company, when they really represent a number of different firms.

Sun Microsystems designs breakthrough computers. The brains inside, the semiconductors, are manufactured at other firms. Sun does not regard these semiconductor firms as vendors, but as partners. Designs are often started years in advance. Collaboration is active between engineers at Sun and their chip partners.

Chips and boards are integrated into computers by Sun manufacturing partners such as Celestica. When Sun places an order, the order is electronically forwarded to Celestica. Celestica is part of the virtual Sun team. Celestica builds the computer, and then ships it to the Sun customer with the Sun logo on the computer and on the shipping box.

Celestica was number one in *Business Week* ranking of the top 100 information technology firms. Celestica is a world leader in Electronics Manufacturing Services (EMS). It manufacturers many of the brand-name products which your corporation uses to run its business. Celestica is the ultimate in cost leadership, relentlessly keeping its operating margin under 4%.

If a Sun customer needs service, 800-USA4SUN is dialed. A technical support person listens to the customer, and diagnoses the likely problem. If the problem cannot be resolved on the phone, a service engineer is dispatched who may work for a separate service organization (another virtual team member). The independent service engineer presents a Sun business card and ID badge.

The equipment may be leased from Sun, even though GE Capital (another virtual team member) is really handling the financing. The final customer always feels that they are dealing with Sun Microsystems. The computers all have Sun's logo. All correspondence from orders, to leases, to shipping documents all carry Sun's logo. Sun, like all successful virtual corporations, shows one face to the customer, with no finger-pointing.

Lightspeed Response

Lightspeed response involves responding to your customer faster and better than all your competitors. Your best customers see you as part of their virtual teams. Customers want to reach your people immediately. They want their computer systems linked to yours for automatic information and response. Customers want to work at the speed of light.

QLogic is a revenue rocket. *Fortune* Magazine recognizes it as one of the 20 fastest growing companies. For several years, this corporation has averaged growth that exceeds 100% per year. QLogic has expanded from making specialized electronic components, to being a leader in computer storage products.

QLogic's biggest customer is Sun Microsystems. QLogic is another important player on Sun's virtual team. Sun engineers in northern California and in Massachusetts work closely with QLogic engineers in southern California and Minnesota. Large documents are exchanged securely over the Internet. These documents can be marked with suggestions, discussed with instant messaging and improved in real time. Electronic design files are exchanged. Voice and video conference calls pull virtual teams together. In this new way of working, geographies and time zones blur. QLogic delivers lightspeed response.

When designs are done, operations management at QLogic work closely with their counterparts at Sun. Forecasts are shared. Computers systems are linked across the Internet, so that QLogic does not ship a product until needed by Sun.

Lightspeed 5^3

You can increase revenues and build customer relationships when every salesperson implements a 5x5x5 lightspeed plan:

- ✓ **Select your 5 most important customers.**
- ✓ **Select the 5 most important decision makers and influencers for each of those customers.**
- ✓ **Give each person 5 ways to reach you for lightspeed response such as your cell phone, your home phone, your alphanumeric pager, your instant message ID, and your email.**

QLogic OEM Director Pohan Chiang succeeds by building lifetime customer relationships with lightspeed response. He gets the right QLogic people working with the right customer people at the right times. He personally believes in lightspeed response. Pohan gives Sun executives and managers his cell phone number and his home phone number. They can send an instant message to his alphanumeric pager. When a product has a "bug," Pohan convinces his engineers to get on a plane and live with the Sun engineers until the problem is solved.

As QLogic has earned the confidence of Sun, they have progressed from just making ASIC chips, to also making the complete boards that included the chips. Thus *the partnership* has expanded to making entire switches that include boards and chips. When Sun has a problem, QLogic expands its business model to meet the need, most recently by expanding into storage software. QLogic's relationship with Sun has expanded from chip supplier to product set provider to business partner.

Sales Teams

Sales teams manage lifetime customer relationships. Teams can vary from two people to 200. Team member job titles can include:

- ✓ **Global Account Executive**
- ✓ **Sales Account Executive**
- ✓ **Inside Sales**
- ✓ **Pre-Sales Engineer**
- ✓ **Customer Support**

Sun Area Vice President, Joe Womack, sees investments in strategic account teams as key to his $2 billion in area sales: "In the old days, sales focused on representing their company. Today sales act like executives who are focused on helping customers make money, cut costs, and enhance relationships with customer stakeholders. Salespeople are now focused on relationships, trust, communication, and process."

How do these sales teams implement customer communication and lightspeed response?: "Each of our strategic customers from General Motors to McDonald's has its own culture," continues Vice President Womack, "You need to use a mix of personal, telephone, and electronic communication that fits the customer's culture. Face-to-face is the most customer intimate, and the most expensive way to communicate. Telephone is more intimate, perfect for call center sales and support, and mid-range in cost. Electronic, such as email and eBusiness, is the least personal, but carries the lowest costs. Sales teams must balance customer intimacy with efficiency."

Coke Adds Life at IBM

Coca-Cola is a very important customer to IBM. Coca-Cola's lifetime value to IBM is billions of dollars. IBM makes information technology a tool to help Coke grow its global market-share one country at a time, and one bottle at a time.

IBM has over 100 people on-site at Coca-Cola. At one point, IBM's global account executive was the son-in-law of Coca-Cola's Chairman of the Board. That is truly customer intimacy.

Onsite sales teams ideally become part of the customer's virtual team. They facilitate lightspeed response. They create major competitive barriers.

Account Executives

Account Executives (AEs) are the salespeople responsible for building lifetime customer relationships. For a given customer, an account executive must simultaneously build quarterly revenue, ensure customer delight, and establish a relationship that is profitable for their corporation and the customer. The role of the AE is strategic, not transactional.

AEs evaluate all long-term opportunities with a customer. They develop a long-term plan, such as three years, to build the relationship. They look for opportunities to partner with a customer. They look for joint venture opportunities.

Account Executives focus on building corporate and personal relationships. They are most valuable for working face-to-face with the customer. AEs build relationships between their corporation's people and the customer's people at all levels.

AEs should be freed from all order processing. Instead, let customers use eCommerce, supply-chain integration, and inside salespeople. AEs are compensated for all orders from their accounts without touching any of them. Account Executives focus on large, high-profit sales. When asked how often a salesperson should touch an order, Sun's Joe Womack gave an instant response, "Never."

Inside Sales and Customer Support

Inside salespeople live on the telephone. These jobs are often based in sophisticated call centers, where they can work as teams handling calls from customers, and calls to customers. Empower inside salespeople to provide lightspeed response for all tactical issues from taking orders to tracking delivery. Have inside salespeople work as a team with account executives.

Lifetime customer relationships are built on the ongoing support of customers. Support involves delivering what is ordered. It involves exceeding customer expectations. Great support includes lightspeed response to inevitable problems. Great support is the foundation of profits. Securing an initial order from a customer is time consuming and expensive. Profits are built on years of reoccurring business with lifetime customers.

Customer support is increasingly offered to give customers choices about how and when they interact. Sometimes a face-to-face meeting is preferred with someone who smiles, cares and is competent. Other times a to-the-point conversation is desired with an executive who can break the rules on the spot. Increasingly customers prefer to use the telephone and the Internet for some, or all, of their issues. Give your customers multiple touchpoints.

Nordstrom is a retailer with a good reputation for building lifetime customer relationships. Competent people are ready to help you in their stores. These people remember their best customers and what they want. Nordstrom people stay friendly if a customer needs help with exchanging or returning merchandise.

Customer expectations have increased. Nordstrom, like all retailers, must respond to customers who want help 24 hours each day, 7 days per week. Retailers cannot afford to have stores open all night. Retailers must extend support to customers with telephone call centers and a helpful Internet site.

When a customer calls Nordstrom, they are not asked to go through endless voice menus, and then wait 20 minutes listening to an endless recording about how much the company cares. A live person greets callers within seconds. The person in the call center is knowledgeable. The customer support person has a computer system to view the customer relationship. Shipments can be traced. Returns can be handled.

Some customers prefer the speed of the Internet to dialogues with people. Nordstrom offers a website that is easy to navigate, rich in content, includes sizing guidelines, gift recommendation tools, and answers to common customer questions. Email feedback is invited, is tracked to resolution, and customers get their questions answered in a quick and easy manner.

Instant Messaging is welcomed in dealing with anything from underwear to questions about personal beauty transformations. Cinderella used to get help from some furry mice, now she gets it with just one mouse-click.

If an item is purchased on the Internet, it is shipped with easy to follow directions on making returns and exchanges. Nordstrom brands this "Super Easy Returns," and lives up to the promise. Nordstrom offers customers lightspeed response.

Customer support is being embedded into devices. The smart refrigerator can monitor itself, predict a future failure of the icemaker, and then connect across the Internet to schedule a repair.

Lifetime Customer Value

Normally, 20% of your customers generate 80% of your profits. With these treasured customers, we must respond with the values that they expect. Customers want us to be the best with creative products, customer intimate services or operationally efficient cost savings. We must partner with our best customers. We must move with lightspeed response.

The year 2000 started with AOL stunning the business world in buying media giant Time Warner for $165 billion. How could an upstart Internet service provider buy one of the world's largest companies? The stock market valued AOL's customers at $7,455 each, over twice the value of a Time Warner customer. Investors figured that AOL customers would stay loyal, and periodically spend more monthly with AOL. Investors were less confident about Time Warner customer loyalty to its TV stations, magazines, and newspapers.

In her wonderful book, *The Customer Revolution,* Patricia Seybold makes a convincing case that the value of companies will increasingly be measured by the lifetime value of their customer relationships. Value is measured by your number of existing customers, your ability to retain them, and by the lifetime value of customer profits. Value is also measured by these factors for future customers.

Data Warehouse

A data warehouse extracts information from databases used for transactions, such as order entry and accounting. A data warehouse also includes information that helps salespeople, customer support, and customer websites. A data warehouse organizes the information so that people can more quickly find what is needed. A data warehouse helps organize marketing campaigns.

MCI uses inside sales teams in call centers to grow share in specific markets. One of MCI's small business sales groups had a classic problem — they could not get accurate information about customers. This information was buried in older accounting systems, inaccessible to the salespeople. It was so bad, that MCI paid millions to rent and buy mailing lists from outside companies.

MCI built a data warehouse of small business information. MCI sales representatives can easily find specific types of customers. For example, the data warehouse allows a sales representative to find retailers in New Jersey with 4 to 8 phone lines currently using AT&T long distance services. Sales reps can quickly capitalize on marketing campaigns.

MCI built a data warehouse with 48 million customer records. MCI made the data warehouse easy for salespeople to use by letting them access information "point and click" using their Internet browser. Sales doubled for the small business sales team at MCI. They have saved millions by not buying mail lists for each new campaign. Sales, marketing, and service can now work together.

CRM

Customer Relationship Management (CRM) is the strategies, processes, and software applications that enable people to work as a team in sales and with the support of customers. CRM uses a data warehouse, and adds information to it. eCRM gives customers Web access to these applications and information.

Hewlett-Packard (HP) commands the number-two slot among computer companies worldwide. Dell is number one in volume of computers. HP is reinventing itself to look more like customer intimate leader IBM. CRM will help HP be more customer intimate.

Building a strong relationship with the customer requires a streamlined and consistent response from everyone in a corporation. It also requires a single view of the customer:

"With our rapid rate of growth, we found ourselves with seven legacy forecasting systems," stated Mike Overly, CRM implementation manager at HP. "Our sales reps make commitments on what they expect to bring in every month. All of that information is then rolled up to the worldwide manager, who tries to forecast with reasonable accuracy. Unfortunately, it was impossible for the manager to push a button and get an accurate forecast or a true view of the customer. It was all done instead via word of mouth and e-mail, so it was a very disjointed process."

"Our main objective was to create an industry leading customer experience. We wanted to delight our customers — regardless of the touchpoint," said Overly. "We wanted to make the sales force more productive and increase revenues while reducing costs."

✓ **Being able to integrate the front office with the back office was crucial.**

HP implemented CRM software applications for sales, marketing, and call centers. The system is for 11,000 sales reps and their field team worldwide. One important goal: "A sales manager will be able to view up-to-the-minute sales and order information, get an accurate picture of any current service issues, and determine which marketing events our customers have recently attended."

Hewlett-Packard is convinced that its investment will pay off globally: "We expect to see an increase in productivity, with one measure being the reduced number of 'phone tag' calls that sales reps must make," described Overly. "Our CRM business processes will provide a consistent customer experience—regardless of the touchpoint—it will give account managers a much more accurate feel for what's happening with our customers. With, our CRM solution, we'll know much more about each customer. And our ability to sell solutions will increase significantly as a result of this single view of the customer."

Summary

Create lifetime customers with lightspeed response. For major global customers, the response should be from a coordinated team of an account executive, technical specialists, and call center specialists. For many customers, it is channel partners with similar teams who provide the sales and support. Sales and service teams coordinate with CRM, and other forms of comprehensive information. This information, CRM, and the people who work its strategies, are all available to the customer from a variety of touchpoints.

Customers often want to interact with people. At times, they want to deal directly with the information and ordering systems. The Internet has made this possible 24 hours daily, seven days each week. In the next chapter, we will see how eCommerce has impacted the sales process, channel partners, and customers.

Executive Action

➤ Establish a customer advisory council.

➤ For top customers, ask your sales team for a plan to make the customer a partner.

➤ For customers strategic to your future, arrange for executive meetings.

➤ For customers that do not fit your leadership model, or who are marginally profitable, lower sales coverage, lower sales costs, and shrink their discounts.

➤ For customers that do not fit your core competencies, or who are unprofitable, end the relationship.

Sales Action

➤ Implement a 5x5x5 lightspeed plan.

➤ Read customer annual reports, executive speeches, articles, and news for strategic customer directions and vision.

➤ Build a close working sales team with regular informal fun activities. Celebrate small success, and major successes will follow.

➤ Plan a meeting with your top customer executives and your other executives to explore a partnership or joint venture.

11

Did eCommerce Change Sales?

> **It is not all or nothing. Sometimes your customers want to deal with a real person. Other times, they want to buy on the Internet.**

ECommerce is defined as "transactions made on the Internet." A broader definition would be "using the Internet to facilitate commerce." There is no magic in doing eCommerce, although there is some magic in doing it better than all your competitors. There is real magic in making eCommerce integral to your total approach to sales and distribution channels.

Let us look at how established companies use eCommerce to accelerate revenue and take business from competition. We examine how eCommerce fits in with direct sales, channels, and supply-chain partners. Forecasts that eCommerce will fail are wrong. Forecasts that eCommerce will disintermediate and eliminate channel partners are also wrong.

The Super Bowl in year 2000 was ultimately a competition of eCommerce startups outspending each other on million dollar ads. The "Buzz" was more important than the "brand" for many young advertisers. While many investors placed big orders for Pets.com, and Webvan, others focused on fundamentals. Investors looked for value leadership, not confused business models. They questioned the sustainable competitive advantage of these firms. They asked how these firms would ever become profitable.

In 2001, Pets.com, Webvan, and hundreds of dot-com startups were bankrupt. In that same year, the total business done on the Internet doubled. eCommerce will exceed $6 trillion dollars in 2004, according to respected forecasters.

eCommerce

ECommerce is commerce that is facilitated by online networks, including the Internet. It includes business-to-business (B2B) and business-to-consumer (B2C) transactions.

A bunch of kids fresh out of college started the biggest change in sales and distribution channels since the Industrial Revolution. They started giving away a breakthrough software package called Netscape Navigator. Soon more people were using it than industry leader Microsoft's two best operating systems — NT and Windows 95.

Netscape went public with their stock, and it immediately was worth several billion dollars. Netscape forced Microsoft to successfully reinvent itself. Microsoft's Internet Explorer was so successful that Netscape struggled to hold market share and make money. AOL bought Netscape to acquire Netcenter, a popular portal that customers use for searches, calendar sharing, collaboration, and commerce. In buying Netscape, AOL also secured technology to extend its reach to businesses, TV watchers, and users of small and portable devices.

ECommerce has permanently changed the rules. Customers, who spent hours scouring the shopping malls for hot products and hot prices, now spend minutes finding hotter products at hotter prices on the Net.

Competition is Everywhere

You now have ten times more competition than before eCommerce became popular. That competition is coming at you from all over the world.

If you are selling flowers, in the past you worried about the flower stand around the corner. Now you worry about flowers.com and other online sellers shipping from everywhere to everywhere. Your former wholesalers are now your competitors. What has happened to flowers has happened to those selling music, travel tickets, financial services, industrial goods, electronics and so on.

Distribution channels reinvented

What does this explosion do to distribution channels? Thousands of players in the software distribution supply chain reinvented themselves, or went out of business. The old rule was for a software developer to sell to a stocking distributor who sold to a software reseller who sold to a customer. The new rule is to give away the early "beta" releases and hope that the new software would offer major improvements that caught competitors flatfooted. Race to get millions of users and then make the software work. Software products are now shipped electronically over the Internet.

For a customer with 10,000 employees, one download, and paying for one corporate license, replaces the whole chain of shipping 10,000 boxes of software.

The new model of eCommerce and Electronic Software Distribution (ESD) has moved the industry to "competing on Internet time," as Michael Cusumano and David Yoffee describe in their excellent book of the same name. The revolution is being extended to anything that was published in other media: Magazines, newspapers, movies, music, research reports, games, content, manuals, and training. There is a race to deliver the published products on the Internet, capture market share, and then turn the market into paid subscribers. If a publisher is really good, they can even make money at this. Eventually.

Best Practices in eCommerce

Your customers need to experience excellence in the "Four Cs" of best practices in eCommerce:

- ✓ **Content**
- ✓ **Customization**
- ✓ **Commerce**
- ✓ **Collaboration**

Content

One of your first Web-browsing experiences was looking at "brochureware." A company literally took its brochures and displayed them on the Internet. Increasingly customers get the information that they need. Websites are organized to let you search and get summary information, then details if you desire. With each mouse-click you can "drill down" to deeper knowledge. You can type in key words and search for what you want. Product catalogues are organized for these searches. Good ones offer various ways to search and find the right products, and the right answers.

Publishers now put their newspapers and magazines on the Internet, or face declining audiences. Movies and e-learning are moving to the Internet as more people have the high-speed access necessary for full-motion video.

Customers should be empowered to get immediate content that helps them use your products and services. Extensive help, technical manuals, self-service, questions-and-answers are all made available on the Internet. Content excellence makes for happy customers and lower support costs.

Commerce

Over one trillion dollars of transactions are completed on the Internet. A good Internet site makes it easy for people to buy. Most buying is done business-to-business (B2B), where credit lines are established, and credit cards are not necessary.

Any corporation which values its selling partners needs to carefully consider displaying product pricing on its website. If a selling partner spends six months developing a sale, and the potential customer then buys at the manufacturer's website at a 20% discount, the selling partner may stop representing the manufacturer. Many partner-friendly sites do not show prices. The sites provide rich content, and search engines that help customers link to partners.

A compromise website approach is to only display list prices, and never undercut partners with discounts. For many, the best approach is to give key customers, and partners, distinct log-ins and password access to price information. Each customer can see his or her own negotiated prices, special configurations, and pre-approved logistics. Prices and discounts are never visible to the casual buying public.

SciQuest is popular with lab technicians because it makes it easy to buy. Chemists can search in a variety of ways for products, including by category, maker or key word. They can bookmark favorites. When they are on the Web order form, they can still get more information. They can even send a note to the supplier. Technicians can save frequent orders, for one-mouse click buying. Yes, they can also talk to a live person.

Configuration software should be implemented to ease the buying of complex products such as computers, network switches, cars, and airplanes. Configuration software, excellent content and customization allow Cisco customers and partners to electronically buy over $10 billion annually.

Amazon is popular with customers because it saves their shopping carts for 90 days. Customers can easily change their mind. They can save shipping addresses for gifts to friends and family. Amazon also provides for one-click buying. A lesson from Amazon is that on the Internet make it easy for customers to buy.

Customization

The Internet makes delivering each person a unique marketing experience possible. Wireless cell phone users can get summary text, and easy navigation, that matches the slower speed of their wireless connection. Increasingly, the Web experience will be tailored to your physical location, such as when you want to find the nearest Starbucks. Most web purchasing and usage will soon be from small wireless devices.

Each person can have a unique experience at the same website. Internet sites have a three-tier architecture. Customers experience the user interface. Behind the scenes are databases that keep profiles about customer Web preferences and past buying patterns. The user interface can also be a window to applications that manage ordering, inventory, customer relationships, supply-chain management and more.

Customers want convenience and privacy. Permission marketing builds trust by empowering customers to reveal, or keep private, information about them. With trust, incentives, convenience and the respect of privacy, many customers will eventually reveal a great deal about their needs, their corporations, preferences, and plans.

One-to-one marketing is followed with 1:1 delivery. At CarPoint, you can have a car built to your precise specifications and delivered to you. At MP3 you can create your perfect music album, and have it downloaded to you while you listen.

Collaboration

Since the beginning of time, sales professionals have understood the importance of dialogue. We ask questions to understand customer needs. We provide feedback. We explain the benefits. We hear problems and try to solve them. This dialogue must exist on the Internet.

Customers should be provided with buttons that initiate instant message exchanges with live people. As voice over the Internet (VOIP) improves, these dialogues can be voice conversations.

Customers like to form special interest communities. If you want to be the number one online travel agent, let business travelers trade ideas, the same for active vacationers, the same for Tahiti lovers, and so on. They will sometimes praise your firm. Sometimes they will complain. You will gain priceless market research.

Yahoo is a popular place to shop because it is a portal. Yahoo provides thousands of special interest communities with the ability to collaborate, get news and links specific to their interest. In turn, its millions of visitors are comfortable with advertisements and shopping links specific to their interest.

Cisco is an excellent provider of collaboration for network engineers. If it is 2 a.m., and a network is down, engineers can find other engineers to help with ideas and insights. Most Cisco customer problems are resolved without any involvement from Cisco. This successful leader empowers customers with Internet help, e-learning, diagnostics and collaboration.

ECommerce provides customers with excellent content, customization, commerce, and collaboration. Behind the scenes are powerful applications that process orders, check inventory, connect to suppliers, and schedule shipping. The eCommerce experience is driven by large databases rich in information about the customers, the products, and the needed information content.

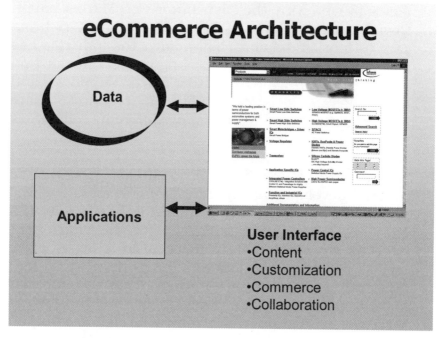

Collaborative eMarket Reshapes Distribution

Automotive parts are a multi-billion dollar business. DaimlerChrysler, Ford Motor Company and General Motors created a giant eMarket for auto parts. The exchange is called Covisint. General Motors purchases over billions of dollars of parts through Covisint each year.

Every major distributor must expand to include the offerings of successful eMarkets including online catalogues, auctioning and private exchanges. Distributors have the competitive advantage of brand, channel loyalty, logistics, inventory, and financial services.

Collaboration is increasingly the decisive factor in who wins the Distributor vs. eMarket battle. Covisint uses collaboration to help automakers bring cars to market sooner. Historically, the industry has faced huge problems in exchanging documents and engineering drawings between parts suppliers and automakers. Covisint provides a platform where formerly incompatible tools of different companies now work together.

Covisint provides this example: "During the product development process, a vehicle team receives direction from marketing to increase the capacity of a glove box. The engineering lead for the instrument panel is given the task to incorporate a larger glove box while maintaining functionality and performance. The engineer learns that the supplier for the glove box door needs to finalize the tool in three weeks to support the vehicle launch deadline.
The modification requires coordination throughout the vehicle program team (engineering, interior styling, human packaging, testing) as well as the supplier's organization. The engineering lead estimates the change will take six weeks to implement with their current process — three weeks longer than the supplier has for final tool modification."

The engineering lead decides to use the Covisint Collaboration Manager tool. He logs on to Covisint and creates a workspace for the Glove Box Modification project. Then, he adds team members, loads the marketing specification documents, and the project-specific documents into the workspace. The team members are notified via e-mail and receive a URL directing them to their workspace.

"In the next three weeks, the team uses Collaboration Manager to review documents, conduct virtual design reviews, and assign and track issues. The team quickly reviews all design decisions and carries out various "what-if" studies. Through the use of a Collaboration Manager, the designer develops a solution for the glove box and uploads the new design on the workspace. The design is approved and the supplier's tool deadline is met."

Amazon vs. Wal-Mart

Avid readers browse at Meg Ryan's fictitious children's bookstore in the movie "You've Got Mail." The big store down the street puts her out of business. Somehow, she is able to open her heart to the big store's owner, Tom Hanks. In real life, the big store is the firm on the defense. They must survive Amazon. Amazon offers readers millions of book titles to browse and purchase from their homes. Instead of fighting endless traffic and desperate searches for parking spaces, readers drive through Amazon's search engine.

Far from Amazon's headquarters in Seattle, is Wal-Mart in Bentonville, Arkansas. Wal-Mart is the most successful retailer in history. Its sales exceed $100 billion. Wal-Mart replaced Sears as the household name in shopping for most Americans. It started with a single store in Arkansas. Wal-Mart did a better job of listening to its customers. It also did a better job of using technology.

Wal-Mart captures customers' buying patterns in a sophisticated data warehouse. The data warehouse allows managers to focus on what to stock, what to promote and what to sell. In fact, Wal-Mart has over 40 programs, which it considers critical to its success, including data warehousing, supply chain management, customer service and point-of-purchase systems.

Wal-Mart's use of technology is so sophisticated that a supplier like Coca-Cola can look at the sales and inventory of any store, then replenish the stock. Including key suppliers across private networks is a growing trend in eCommerce.

Amazon.com got Wal-Mart's attention when it hired Richard Dalzell, Wal-Mart's Vice President of Information Systems (IS). Dalzell had been a brilliant technology architect and leader at Wal-Mart. When little Amazon tried to recruit him, he replied: "It would take an atomic bomb to get my family out of Arkansas." 125,000 stock options in Amazon became that atomic bomb, and Dalzell joined Amazon.

Following Dalzell, one bright IS person after another left Wal-Mart for Amazon. On October 16, 1998, Wal-Mart dropped its own atomic bomb. It filed suit against Amazon. Dark accusations include theft of trade secrets. With both sides facing years of an expensive and very public lawsuit, they settled out of court. The battle is now in the market place.

Yes, Wal-Mart is concerned with losing valuable employees. Protecting trade secrets is also important. Wal-Mart's memory of toppling the giant Sears may cause Wal-Mart to look at Amazon with greater alarm. If Amazon can change the way people shop, Wal-Mart could be history. Wal-Mart must make multi-million dollar investments to reach a new community. It must build a "click and mortar" business that best meets the needs of its customers.

Amazon extends its reach into a new community with one click. It can do business for a fraction of the cost of Wal-Mart stores and other traditional retailers. Amazon is open 24 hours daily, every day of the year. Amazon is one click away, not one town away. The "atomic bomb" quote was prophetic. This is war.

Partner Website

You can leverage the Internet to get big channel results on a tight budget. Leverage comes from a separate website for channel partners. They access it with their own password. If you are a larger corporation, then you are ready to take the next step and have tighter integration with your distributors and key partners across private extranets with these partners. Increasingly, online configuring, pricing and ordering will be tightly integrated across the two-tiered supply chain.

A partner website is rich in tools, files, web-based learning, support and collaboration between you and your partners. It includes all your brochures in digital form. It includes slide presentations, proposal libraries, customer success stories and more. It packages complete marketing programs in digital form so that your partners can spend their money to promote your products and services. If you utilize marketing development funds (MDF), then the entire program is streamlined and uses this site. Make it easy for partners to configure, price and propose solutions that include your products and services.

Integrate this e-learning with mentors inside your company. Provide extensive 24/7 support. Provide for collaboration with and between partners. Enable them to use various email and instant messaging clients.

Supply Chain Collaboration

Wal-Mart has trusting relationships with its key suppliers that includes letting those suppliers into Wal-Mart's critical information systems. Suppliers can look at sales details in any store, at any time, and move quickly to replenish stock. They can learn from sales trends, and introduce better products and promotions. Wal-Mart partners with the top firms from whom it buys products.

Celestica uses supply-chain technology to keep operating margins under 4%. Celestica invested $60 million into computer systems, supply-chain, and database software to handle the $8 billion worth of parts that the company bought in 2000 for its plants, located in 12 countries. The $60 million investment rapidly paid for itself by lowering inventory cost. A supply-chain SWAT team at Celestica sees bloated inventory in real time, and uses the company's buying power to get suppliers to roll back orders.

Summary

Yes, eCommerce has permanently changed sales. Intelligently implemented, eCommerce electronically links all partners with PRM. Your rich product information, marketing campaigns, sales tools, and technical knowledge are immediately available to partners. Poorly implemented, eCommerce makes publicly visible discounted prices that alienate your channel partners. This issue will be examined more closely in the next chapter.

Effective eCommerce builds lifetime customers and partners with lightspeed electronic response and multiple touchpoints. eCommerce is rich in content, commerce, customization, and collaboration.

PRM and collaboration provides tools for close working relationships between partners and your sales force. The challenging aspect is the delicate human relationships that can create sales leverage, not conflict. This is the subject of our next chapter.

Executive Action

➢ Protect channel partners by displaying prices and discounts only to customers with private log-ins and passwords.

➢ Improve eCommerce by allowing customers to electronically order through their purchasing systems or private websites.

➢ Integrate your demand-chain with your enterprise applications and databases.

Sales Action

➢ Free your valuable sales time. Train your customers to place all orders electronically.

➢ For your top 5 customers, sell your company and your customers on having a private website and extranet for each customer.

➢ Use the Internet for lightspeed response with lifetime customers.

12

Sales Leverage not Partner Conflict

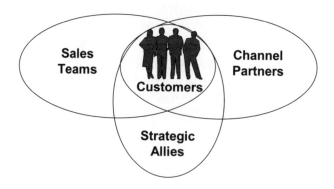

Achieve competitive advantage by taking the customers' experience to the next level. Empower customers with the flexibility of using multiple channels for multiple needs. Provide customers with the convenience of multiple touchpoints. Encouraging everyone to work as a team with the right coverage models, compensation, communications and other customer relationship management. Continued growth depends on using all of these effectively. You must fine-tune the synergy between direct sales teams, channel partners, and eCommerce.

Ability is the art of getting credit for all the home runs somebody else hits.
— **Casey Stengel**

The Transformation of IBM

Take a look back at IBM. In its early years, most IBM revenue was from hardware sales. IBM's direct sales teams made all sales. Now most of IBM's revenue comes from selling software and services through over 20 different types of channel partners. Beyond this, IBM is allowing key customers to buy products and services electronically. eCommerce is an important part of their new sales model.

IBM is legendary for being personally responsive to its customers. IBM dedicates an account team to each major customer. The team gets involved in their customer's long-range strategies. Rapid response to customer problems is expected. IBM makes heroes of account executives and engineers that sleep on cots at customer sites until problems are resolved.

Historically, IBM customers spent years developing custom software solutions for their businesses. All information and applications ran on mainframes. Users, such as sales reps, had IBM terminals on their desk to access information.

Now, customers want complete solutions. Manufacturing wants a factory floor where hardware and software are designed to move an inventory item to the right place at the right time. The manufacturing group wants suppliers to have added parts inventory only at the precise moment needed.

Sales management wants more productivity from reps with notebook computers with special software and PC cards.

IBM's customers want account managers and technical people to guide their strategy. Customers want to buy their IBM PCs from competing corporate resellers who can provide overnight delivery of PCs assembled with hardware and software from many companies loaded and properly working. Two-tiered distribution is needed to ensure that everything is available for the resellers.

Customers will not buy IBM computers unless the best application software is available for these computers. IBM goes to great lengths to have solid working relationships with strategic alliance partners such as SAP, Oracle, Siebel, and PeopleSoft. Just-in-time inventory solutions require that IBM form alliances with Electronic Data Interchange (EDI) vendors and supply-chain leaders such as I2 and SAP. Tracking movement in the factory floor means compatibility partnerships with bar code vendors.

IBM has sales channels to ensure that customers get whole solutions. IBM also has channels to control total cost of sales. IBM channels include direct sales, inside sales, OEM, VAR (value-added resellers), solution integrators, corporate resellers, third party maintenance organizations, direct marketing firms, two-tiered distribution, network providers, EDI, application software firms, Internet service providers, and application service providers.

All companies, not just IBM, have shifted their strategies. All top competitors now use:

✓ **Direct Sales Teams**
✓ **Channel Sales**
✓ **Strategic Alliances**
✓ **eCommerce**

Which Sales Approach Should a Company Emphasize?

	Sales Teams	Channel Partners	Internet
Customer	**Direct Sales Team**	Value	24x7 Support
Creative	Direct Sales Team	**Value then Volume**	1st to Market 1st to Segment Leadership
Cost	Call Center	Volume	**eCommerce**

Continued growth depends on using all sales channels effectively. To be a leader, you must have sales leverage. You must fine-tune the synergy between direct sales teams, channel partners, and eCommerce.

This is illustrated by looking at the battle between HP and Dell. Dell is a leader in eCommerce. They make it easy for customers to visit their website *www.dell.com*, learn about products, and then place orders. Customers can then track delivery electronically. Dell extends its eCommerce success by linking with its key suppliers through the Internet.

HP and Compaq merged in 2002 to try and unseat market leader Dell. Compaq had tried to copy Dell's eCommerce success. When Compaq started taking orders at compaq.com, major Compaq channel partners reacted as if this were a declaration of war. Cost leaders such as Tech Data, Ingram, and SBS wanted to control all Compaq sales, instead of fighting with Compaq to take the orders.

The battle changed market leadership. There was a time when the number one selling PC through channels was Compaq. Now it is the "white box," which is the industry's code for PCs that are custom made and privately branded by the providing resellers. Ingram, the world's largest computer distributor, could not afford to gamble its $30 billion annual sales by assuming that Compaq would continue to sell through distribution. Ingram became the world's largest provider of "white boxes". Compaq and Ingram declared war on each other. Like a fighting couple that wanted to give a good public appearance, they tried to hide this.

Tech Data, the world's number two computer distributor also moved to expand with private label PC assembly and distribution. Tech Data aggressively used eCommerce in a secure private network with thousands of computer resellers. Tech Data made it easy for resellers to configure, finance, order, and track shipments of computers custom assembled from over 100 thousand line-items.

Compaq bought shopping.com, a major Internet-only retailer. Compaq sold through shopping.com in direct competition with its other resellers. Thousands of resellers threatened to stop selling Compaq all together. In response, Compaq stopped selling its popular Presario through Internet-only retailers. Compaq moved to sell differentiated and branded products through different channels.

How about the thousands of resellers that made Hewlett-Packard (HP) (and Compaq), Ingram, and Tech Data into multi-billion dollar success stories? Some resellers are trying to differentiate themselves with low-cost products. Others are positioning themselves as solution integrators with strong professional service capabilities. Hundreds have tried selling HP and private brands through their own web sites. Customers can quickly compare prices. Profit margins fall to zero. Resellers competing on price start going out of business.

How does HP now stop the onslaught from Dell, but not alienate channel partners? HP must find the right sales leverage model. For example, when HP provides eCommerce systems for its channel partners, it is acting as a friend, not a competitor. HP avoids conflict when it provides a direct sales team for a major customer, then only accepts customer orders through channel partners. HP is continually adjusting its direct sales, channel, and eCommerce strategy.

You achieve maximum sales and profits by driving sales in three dimensions: direct sales, strategic partners, and eCommerce.

Customers Select Channels and Teams

It is tempting to put customers in boxes. The problem is that customers do not want to be in boxes.

Channel organizations often drive financial managers crazy. The financial people dutifully try to maximize profits by recommending that only large customers be supported with the expensive investment of direct account teams, mid-sized customers be supported with channels of distribution, and small customers only buy with low-cost eCommerce.

When major customers also buy from channel partners, there appears to be significant waste. Two organizations are running up costs, commissions, and even requiring revenue reconciliation by the financial people. Small customers increase costs when they buy from channel partners then call the product creator for technical help.

Financial giant Citicorp expects IBM to have a direct team that lives with its mission critical mainframe systems. Citicorp prefers to buy kiosks from IBM partners who can then integrate them with touch screens, specialized software, networking, and support. Citicorp will buy electronically when it wants, or face-to-face with an IBM Vice President when it wants. If IBM does not like this approach, HP and Sun Microsystems account executives and partners are only a phone call away.

The solution to these challenges is to profitably give customers what they want. Our mission is to have a deep understanding of the needs of our final customers. We provide them with the channel and sales team options to meet their needs. We manage our profitability in the contracts we have with customers, and the value and support commitments we have with our channel partners. We improve efficiency and profitability by using eCommerce and eChannels. The customer benefits with multiple channels and multiple touchpoints.

Multiple Touchpoints

Customers are quickly frustrated with an organization that looks like a chain of islands. A customer must start over with each island, repeating account numbers, problems, and information that is isolated in another island. Well-run organizations use technology and knowledge to give the customer consistent access to support across all touchpoints. The best organizations extend these multiple touchpoints to their channel partners.

Customers of Charles Schwab have the choice of how they want to interact with this financial services leader. Many customers normally use a Web browser to research investments and place orders. A person can start a complex international trade on the website, telephone a call center, and then be connected with an international specialist. That specialist can view the customer's database, and help them complete the transaction.

Another customer may transfer their pension account into a Schwab IRA by visiting a live person at a Schwab office. That customer is empowered to manage the account online when they want, talk to a competent specialist when needed, receive wireless alerts to their cell phone, and place trades through their palm computer 24 hours daily. Schwab customers have many touchpoints supported by common databases and common applications.

Independent financial advisors advise many Schwab customers. The same 24/7 support is available to these advisors.

Schwab uses eCommerce to control sales cost and give customers more touchpoints. Schwab does not force customers into a box. Customers can interact directly with a Schwab person by phone or in person. Customers can work through independent advisors when appropriate. Customers select the personal or technology approach that best meets their needs at a given moment.

Summary

Sales leverage is the result of profitably responding to customer needs. Channel partners who can provide a variety of complementary products and services can better serve most customers. A small business may be an important customer for a local channel partner that meets many of the businesses needs. That same small business may not be profitable for a remote large corporation to handle directly.

Channel conflict often occurs when competing for the business of large organizations. When these major customers create bidding wars for volume sales, organizations must directly compete for the business or they will lose. When these large organizations need specialized services and integrated solutions, then direct sales teams should work closely with partners who add value for the customer.

The future is exciting for sales and marketing professionals. They will work more closely with customers than ever before. Customers will have more knowledge and more power. The next chapter outlines the future of sales, and provides guidelines about what should be implemented today.

Executive Action

➢ Provide customers with the flexibility of using multiple channels for multiple needs.

➢ Provide customers with the convenience of multiple touchpoints.

➢ Have a plan to have inside and outside sales closely working together using common systems and a common database.

➢ For major accounts, ensure that your sales team is compensation neutral regardless of whether an order is placed directly, or through a channel partner.

Sales Action

➢ Invite your best partners to planning sessions with your major account direct sales teams.

➢ Encourage partners to invite major account direct sales teams to fun off-site activities. Build teams.

➢ Ensure that there is publicity and credit to all the people, when direct sales and partners work together and achieve customer success.

13

The Future of Sales

> **Customers now have more knowledge and power. Plan for a new level of integrated relationship management across the demand-chain. Rethink the role of sales.**

✓ If you do not know where you are going, any road will get you there. Conversely, if you plan for different future scenarios, you will develop flexible and farsighted plans that prepare you for tomorrow.

Knowledge Without Boundaries

It has never been easy to be a channel or marketing executive. From headquarters, it is difficult to see the "frontline" battles and sales. You do not know if your products are flying off the shelves of your distributors and retailers, or just sitting there collecting dust. You cannot forecast, focus promotions, and create sales campaigns unless you know.

Marketing executives could cut their budget in half, if they only knew which half was not effective.

Detailed knowledge is required. They need detailed visibility to the final customer.

Imagine detailed information about every sale of your product: The name of the final user, why they bought it, and what worked in the sales process. With a knowledge-base of this type of information, there will be an automatic updating of forecasts, automated revision of production plans, and revised orders sent to suppliers. Corporations will ship hot products while they are still hot.

We will have ten times the knowledge that we have now because of the eCommerce, relationship-management, and data warehousing outlined in this book. When your channel partner pursues a sale with a final customer, that knowledge will be integrated into the partner's customer relationship management (CRM) system, and their databases. When an order is placed, their enterprise resource applications will be updated.

You will rapidly know which marketing and sales campaigns work, so that you can "fine tune" them, and use them with other channel partners. You will know what does not work, so that you can quickly cut your loses, and make better investments.

This electronic integration of the demand and supply chain will allow you and your partners to see the big picture. You will soon have far greater knowledge about your partners and end-customers.

Enlightened and Empowered Customers

The year is 2010. Cinderella has been invited to a formal ball. She is beside herself with excitement. The invitation is from Charm, who everyone considers to be a total prince. Her mean sisters load her with chores, lie about house rule violations, and get Cinderella grounded. No ball. No prince. You can visualize the bleak picture.

Undaunted, Cinderella logs-on to a family legal clinic, secures an injunction which permits her to attend the ball, orders a new wardrobe from Nordstrom, has the Carriage Limo service pick her up, and pays for it all with her mean sister's electronic bank account (Cinderella installed a spy utility in her sister's Internet browser). Using Google's advanced search mechanism, Cinderella researches Charm's history, interest, and preferences. Her dialogue software application builds a recommended set of questions and intriguing anecdotes for her planned meeting with Charm.

At the ball, Charm is swept off his feet by the incredible conversation and shared interest he has with Cinderella. They agree to meet for a follow-up lunch. The restaurant voice reservation system is called, and a corner table secured. Cinderella beams her level-one personal information from her wristwatch computer to Charm's. Included are her menu and flower preferences. Cinderella leaves shortly before midnight, and arrives home before the midnight curfew negotiated by her lawyer. The Carriage Limo would have been late due to a navigation computer mouse problem, but the limo sensors anticipated the failure two-hours before it occurred, and automatically downloaded a software patch.

Charm is now full of anticipation about his planned lunch with Cinderella. He reviews her menu and flower preferences, and has his wristwatch computer make appropriate merchant orders. He notices that she did not reveal her home address. Of course, Cinderella could not have him see her at home. What are you going to do when you have mean sisters?

In 2010, Cinderella is our future customer. She is wise, always connected, ready to make immediate purchases, and soon to be half-owner of a very large estate.

Your customers already have a deeper knowledge of your products, services, and competition, than they did a few years ago. There was a time when a competitor in a different country was not a threat. Now your customers can learn about their new product the day it is announced. They can acquire deep knowledge through electronic catalogs, papers, streaming video demonstrations, and e-learning. Customers can talk to inside salespeople around the clock. They can locate all the channel partners.

The balance of power has shifted to the customer. They have the knowledge. Geography is less important. Free trade is just that. Customers can order 24/7.

"Customers have a new level of knowledge and power," observes Sun Vice President Joe Womack. "Sales people must respond with a deeper knowledge of the customer's business. Sales people must add knowledge to be effective at solving a customer's business problems. Salespeople are paid for building long-term, trustworthy relationships. Salespeople are not paid to process orders."

You have customers and market segments aligned to a channel coverage model. Your customers, however, want to buy from whomever they want, whenever they want. Customers may want to bypass channels to gain insights into your future directions. At the early stages of a product lifecycle, they may prefer a solution integrator to your expensive, direct-sales team. They may drop the integrator when they place recurring volume orders, and then try to engage you in a price war with your channels. Customers will increasingly place their orders with the lowest bidder in an online market exchange.

Smart leaders will not fight the enlightened and empowered customer. Market leaders will adjust their channel coverage to meet customers' dynamic needs. The solutions will be better.

Channel models will be continuously "fine-tuned" with an optimal balance of direct sales, partners with various value-disciplines, and efficient eCommerce.

Think Global. Act Mobile.

Enlightened and empowered customers create enormous opportunity. For example, a small consulting firm may only have been visible to local customers. Now the firm can be visible to the world. The global playing field creates a double-edged sword. You have the opportunity to reach far more customers and opportunities. You have much more visible competition.

However, all of this increases the need for implementing Revenue Rocket strategies. Systems must deliver realtime market and customer information. Competitive intelligence is now as important to the corporation as radar is to a military defense system. Firms must be better at differentiating from competition with unique cost efficiencies, creative products, or customer intimacy. They must move faster.

✓ **Think global. Global partners are more important than ever.**

Act mobile. Customers will bring us their problems around the clock. Increasingly, their initial communication will be through a cell phone with integrated email and Web browser. We must empower customers with the online help and support to resolve most problems. We must continue to let them dialogue with real people, when that is their preference. We need to keep them informed on the status of resolving their problem, and simultaneously keep our own team informed.

Similarly, order opportunities now occur 24/7. Major opportunities must get immediate visibility by call center teams and customer teams. Automatic escalation needs to be implemented to make important customer opportunities and problems visible up the management chain.

Envision customers with "always-on" mobile technology. Envision the same for your channel partners and customer teams. Think global. Act mobile.

People Touch People, Not Orders

About 20 years ago, Ken Olsen, founder and then CEO of Digital Equipment, remarked in an interview that his sales force could be eliminated. This sent shockwaves through Digital's global sales force of over ten thousand people. A brilliant engineer from MIT, Ken Olsen, had no use for salespeople. He felt that he could give all customers a catalogue of Digital products, and let them order directly from the company.

In many ways, that was the beginning of the end for Digital. They had grown to be the number-two computer company, and were steadily gaining market share from IBM. Digital had started as a creative leader. They created the minicomputer. Soon, an entire new value-chain developed around their products.

Olsen's vision was correct in some ways and fatally flawed in others. Increasingly, salespeople never touch orders. Customers now have electronic catalogues as near as their Web browsers. Smart companies empower their customers to order 24 hours, daily. They encourage electronic orders. The best customers can even have their computers automatically place orders across supply-chain integrated extranets.

Electronic ordering does not eliminate salespeople. Rather, it frees them to be more effective and add more value. It allows them to focus on building lifetime customer relationships. It frees them to respond to problems and opportunities with lightspeed response.

The best firms have freed account executives from touching orders. When a customer needs help from live person, they are helped by an inside salesperson in a call center. Enlightened firms then give the sales team immediate visibility to all orders, and other customer interaction through a CRM system.

Troubled firms continue to make sales order-processing a required job of the salesperson. They even tie compensation to the salespeople processing orders. This chains salespeople to fax machines, whereas they should be helping customers with important issues and solutions.

Enlightened firms extend electronic ordering to their channel partners with integrated PRM systems. This frees channel partners to focus on providing value-added solutions.

Virtual Teams and Team Nets

Hierarchies are giving way to nets. Be delighted if your competition insists that their sales organization remain rigid. Hope that your competitors always engage the same partners for the same geographies. Delight if they are paper intensive with checkers checking checkers. You gain major competitive advantage by being flexible, and eliminating unnecessary bureaucracy.

Cap Gemini Ernst & Young is a global consulting giant. They pride themselves on organizing teams to meet customer needs. When DaimlerChrysler needed to bring cars to market more quickly and cost-effectively, Cap Gemini Ernst & Young organized a team to go after the business. The team included partners with deep experience with Daimler and Chrysler executives. The team included Europeans and Americans. It included experts in manufacturing, supply-chain integration, and technology.

They won the business and expanded the team to include technology leaders such as IBM, HP, Sun Microsystems, SAP, Oracle, Web Methods, and independent consultants with expertise in applications and technology. The team coordinates with email, instant messaging, collaboration software, and private portals. When the project is complete, team members will join new customer-centric teams.

This is the new age of virtual teams and team nets. Cap Gemini Ernst & Young refers to their approach as an alliance "eco-system," stating: "This is the age of the eco-system, because in a world of such complexity no single business can possibly have all the answers. What matters now is to deliver not simply the best that your own company can offer, but also the sum total of your alliance partners' expertise and experience as well. You must have the ability to select the best from everything now on offer and use them as building blocks for the development of your own solutions."

Not only does Cap Gemini Ernst & Young practice virtual teaming, they help customers to do the same. A big part of their automotive practice is implementing collaborative processes to coordinate everyone in the automotive supply-chain in delivering a unique car to each unique customer.

1:1 Marketing Meets 1:1 Sales

Marketing people have long been jealous of the one-to-one (1:1) relationship that a salesperson has with a customer. The salesperson can create a dialogue. The salesperson can listen, and then tailor their messages and solutions to one customer at a time.

One-to-one marketing is the dream of marketing executives. Soon customers will view TV commercials tailored to their interests. Each person will see a different car commercial. Each will see different apparel being modeled. This dream is becoming a reality. The Internet will converge with TV broadcasting. The largest provider of Internet access and TV programming is already the same company, AOL Time Warner.

Already, customers can view advertisements, including video commercials, on the Internet. With a mouse click, or voice command, the customer can go deeper into the subject. With another click, they can be connected to an inside salesperson that can see what information was just viewed by the customer. CRM and eCommerce technology are increasingly used to provide customers with 1:1 marketing and sales experiences.

Always-on Channels

Channel partners, as well as customers, require a "think global, act mobile" mindset. Sales and support people in your channels will communicate with your firm through a cell phone with integrated email and Web browser. Your channels will be always on. They will do business with always-on suppliers. Put rich information at their fingertips about services, products, problem resolution, order creation, and status. If you better serve your always-on channels, you will take business from slow moving competition. Fail to be the best provider of always-on knowledge, and you are at the mercy of your competition.

If you are now implementing the strategies in this book, then each channel partner will be used for their strengths in the right market segments. Partners will offer the right value. They will be engaged at the best point in the product lifecycle. Each partner will want to receive personalized information. Most will want your help in automatically updating sections of their website, but each in a different way. Each will have unique support requirements. Each will want a different 1:1 experience when working with your firm.

Partner relationship management (PRM) and database technology will be deployed. Partners will see only the information that matches their interest and your relationship with each one. Partners will only see information about products and part numbers for which you have authorized them to sell. Partners will be empowered to change their preferences about how they get authorized information.

Services, Not Products

As global competition and eCommerce intensify price competition, product profit margins fall for channel partners. Increasingly, services are the primary source of profits for channel partners. Services already generate most of the profits of customer intimate leaders. Cost leaders also market branded services, and promote profitable logistic and financial services.

Creative leaders, like Oracle and Siebel generate over 20% of their revenues from their services. The services are critical for customer satisfaction and the creation of complete customer solutions. Custom consulting services lead to new technology, which is then incorporated in next generation products. For many organizations the choice is to fund their own research and development, or have it funded by customer service engagements.

In the future, to succeed in channels you must make your product a platform for channel services. Microsoft is a master at this. They have strong channel loyalty, even though most resellers cannot make any money selling their products. Microsoft channels make their money implementing, integrating, and supporting Microsoft products. Top consultants are billed at over $200 per hour to implement and integrate complex software.

Microsoft spends hundreds of millions of dollars to help its channel partners succeed with Microsoft-centric services. Microsoft provides hundreds of technical certification courses. It brands services, and helps partners promote and deliver these services. The result is over 100,000 global partners of Microsoft with over one million people promoting Microsoft products.

Many products are transforming into services. For millions, *The Wall Street Journal* is no longer a newspaper. Instead, it is an online service that readers customize to deliver specific information realtime to their Web browser or Palm computer. More software is transforming from being a product delivered on a CD to an online service where the latest version of the application can be used.

Surprise

It's difficult to forecast, especially about the future.
— **Yogi Berra**

One large oil, gas, and energy company forecast that in 2050, 20% of its revenue would come from "surprise". The other categories were gasoline, natural gas, coal, wind, and solar power. They wisely expect the unexpected.

Twenty percent is usually too low. 50 years ago, the music industry could have forecasted 80% of its revenue from vinyl records. They would have missed the huge impact of CDs, tape, and Internet downloaded MP3. Looking ahead 50 years, we are likely to overestimate the status quo, and underestimate surprise.

We know that we will be surprised, but do not know how. An understandable response is to ignore surprise. It is understandable to not plan for 50 years, 5 years, or 5 months. Not planning is fatal to a corporation.

Andy Grove, the brilliant, former CEO of Intel, discusses the importance of identifying and responding to "strategic inflection points" in his book, *Only the Paranoid Survive*: "An inflection point occurs where the old strategic picture dissolves and gives way to the new, allowing the business to ascend to new heights. However, if you don't navigate your way through an inflection point, you go through a peak, and, after the peak, the business declines."

We can prepare for the unexpected. We can view dramatic change as an opportunity to reinvent part of our business, and then grow to new heights. We can implement the following:

Radar. Listen to partners and their customers. Join channel partners in their customer visits, because reports of what you shipped to distributors do not tell us the latest thinking of our ultimate customer. Channel partners also resell for your competition. Listen with an open mind, and you will receive an early warning of your problems and your competitors' vulnerabilities.

Future Scenarios. Once a year, retreat. Read what the futurists, research firms, and trade journals forecast. Plan for different scenarios. Plan your response. It helps you to be ready. Sometimes, breakthrough ideas come from this process.

Strategic Inflection Point. The best way to identify a strategic inflection point is with hindsight. Otherwise, it is tough. A PRM system can give you early warning of changing sales trends in your channels. A CRM system can capture changing customer behavior and issues. Debate whether your industry is forming new value-chains around new technology.

Assert Leadership. If you decide that you are at a strategic inflection point, refocus on your creative, cost, or customer intimate leadership. Creative leaders will invest in the new-value chain. Customer intimate leaders will meet with the 20% of their customers who generate 80% of the business and listen to their ideas. Cost leaders will streamline processes, and invest in applications, and the technologies that make them more efficient.

Triage and Outsource. A new season for your business is like a new season in baseball. Your stars need spring training to get back to basics and get in shape. Eliminate bureaucracy that will prevent the reinventing of your business. Focus on your unique competitive advantages. Outsource the rest.

Channel Triage and Investment. In times of significant change, you need to end agreements with channel partners that no longer fit. You will have accumulated resellers who add no value. End these relationships. Add partners who fit your new business model. Add channel partners who create new customer solutions in new market segments.

Market Segment Focus. New technology needs to be nurtured to market segment leadership. Target a market segment where you can be the dominant leader. Create complete solutions that solve major customer problems.

Protect and Expand. Protect each key customer and market segment. Expand service offerings to meet new needs. Expand to dominance of a bigger market.

Summary

The future will be rewarding to those who are tightly linked to customers and partners across seamless, always-on networks. Sales professionals will be free from the mundane so that they can stay focused on their customers and complex customer issues.

Now is the time to be electronically linked to customers and partners. CRM and PRM can be deployed now for team efficiency and customer satisfaction. Corporate sales and marketing tools can be immediately available to partners.

Our imagination creates visions of new ways to sell, new markets, and new technology. A challenge is achieving short-term profits, while investing in the future. In the next chapter, you will see how to protect existing customers and products, while you expand into new opportunities.

Executive Action

➢ Expect surprise. Implement radar and encourage rapid response.

➢ Make integration of systems across the supply and demand chains a top priority with key customers and suppliers.

➢ Increase sales time. Do not have salespeople touch orders.

➢ Think global. Act mobile.

Sales Action

➢ When making sales calls, assume that your top customers know as much about your company, products, and services as you do.

➢ Use your firm's CRM and PRM systems to get inside teams and partners to handle routine actions. Focus on long-term opportunities and your plan to be 300% of your goal.

➢ Empower customers to place online orders with your partners and with your inside salespeople. Do not touch another order.

➢ Leverage your valuable sales time with a Palm computer/cell phone that integrates with your CRM and PRM.

14

Protect and Expand

	Products and Services		
	Existing	Improved	New
Existing Customers		$	
Existing Markets (non-customer)		$	$
New Markets		$	

Investing in Customers, Markets and Products

Your business is like a portfolio of stocks. Invest in the right areas. Most firms should invest about 40% of their marketing, hiring, and product development in protecting and expanding business with existing customers. They should invest another 40% in dominating specific market segments where they can be the number one leader in revenue, profits, and customer satisfaction.

Creative leaders invest 20% in creating new "breakthrough" products using disruptive technology. Customer intimate and cost leaders invest 20% in expanding into new markets.

Use the above product-market matrix. Sort your business between existing, improved, and fundamentally new products. Then further divide your business between existing and new customers and new markets.

You can use this matrix to decide where to invest in growing your business. If you invest in the right areas, the odds are good that you will succeed. Invest in the wrong areas, and you are likely to fail. For example, the area of highest risk is the lower right corner: Introducing new products to new markets. New products are always a risk. The risk of failure is high if you take it to a market where you are unknown, and where you do not understand the customer issues.

Traditionally, the area of lowest risk is in selling existing products to existing customers. Your local grocery store owner carefully tracks what sells, and keeps this on the shelves for his regular customers. Increasingly, it is better to constantly improve products and services, than it is to stand still. If the grocery store does not improve its offerings, customers start drifting to innovative competition.

Investing in growth requires scarce money and talented people to sell, market, and develop new products. You need to invest in the areas that will give you the best return-on-investment.

Growth also involves a delicate balance between building lifetime customers and finding new customers. You find new customers most easily in the market segments where you are established. It takes more time and money to develop new markets. For most businesses, the greatest profits come from constantly improving products and services for existing customers and existing markets.

For example, Home Depot is constantly reviewing which products are selling, and which are sitting on the shelf. It strives to improve its product offerings. Home Depot invests heavily in product improvements. Home Depot will also selectively invest in new breakthrough services, such as installing solar power in San Diego homes. Home Depot focuses heavily on existing customers, and existing markets. It will selectively expand into new countries.

Home Depot does an excellent job of investing in four areas. The following are the four best areas for growth. Each requires a different strategy.

	Products and Services		
	Existing	Improved	New
Existing Customers		**Protect**	
Existing Markets (non-customer)		**Dominate**	**Differentiate**
New Markets		**Expand**	

Protect

Protect your business with existing customers by listening carefully to them, then making improvements. Especially important are the 20% of our customers who generate 80% of our profits.

Building lifetime customer relationships is the purpose of business. Great companies are in a continual dialogue with their customers. Customers suggest new products and services. Leaders look at the suggestions that fit core competencies and that make money, and then implement the suggestions.

Customer input is so important that most firms formalize the process. Customers are surveyed. Customer satisfaction forms are included in packaging. Incentives are offered to customers that register products bought through distribution channels. CRM and data warehousing is used to manage the process, and generate reports. Executives devote time with customers.

Customer perception *is* reality. Sales people, support people, and channel partners are in constant dialogue with customers. Leaders listen carefully to sales channel input. Confused companies kill the messenger.

Many products can be made better by simply improving services. We offer customers the option to pay for 24/7 support. We train our people to better answer questions. We have fun and smile more. We do a better job of building lifetime customers with lightspeed response.

Dominate

Growth is achieved when we dominate market segments. We segment the market. We select the right market segment. We are first to market, and eventually the market leader.

Toyota ranks #1 in *Fortune* magazine's list of companies globally admired for the quality of their products and services. It entered the USA, targeting cost-conscious customers. It worked hard to keep customers happy; the word spread. Potential customers contact Toyota. Leads are captured and sent to Toyota dealers. The dealers help Toyota expand into bigger markets.

Growth with new customers accelerates by being first to market with improved products. For example, Toyota is first to market with its 4-door hybrid electric Prius. Integrated marketing helps whet the appetite of new customers. Buying motives are analyzed. Brands are positioned. Marketing managers develop for each market segment the ideal combination of advertising, public relations, direct response, Internet marketing, events, and promotions. Channels receive all the marketing and sales tools to extend the message, and integrate it with their own service brand.

Toyota promises what it can deliver. Toyota delivers more than it promises. Toyota's quality message has been consistent for years. It listens to customers, and strives to continually improve.

Successful companies attract strategic allies. Allies are involved in co-marketing, and strengthening the value-chain. Market segment leadership is achieved. Leadership expands into larger markets.

Differentiate

Creative leaders invest 20% of their expansion budget in creating new "breakthrough" products using disruptive technology. They succeed by focusing on one market segment at a time, starting with a segment where they currently lead.

In our *Product Life Cycle* chapter, we saw how DaimlerChrysler is taking a "differentiate" strategy with electric vehicles. DaimlerChrysler is first to market with fuel-cell buses. DaimlerChrysler is already the world leader in buses. They are wisely starting from a position of market dominance as they expand with breakthrough innovation.

By starting with buses, they have the support of the entire value-chain of suppliers, channels, and customers. They have deep insight into the market. Visionary customers trust DaimlerChrysler to work through the problems that are inevitable when you are trying to change the world. When DaimlerChrysler achieves market leadership with fuel-cell buses, they will be well positioned to expand into larger markets of trucks and fleet vehicles.

Expand

Customer and cost leaders invest 20% in expanding into new markets.

Customer and cost leaders invest heavily in keeping customers happy. They do not make big bets in research and development. Most companies can best grow by expanding into larger markets. They expand by adopting existing products to the needs of bigger markets. They improve services to meet the larger market needs.

Channel partners and strategic allies are the key players when you expand into a new market. Although you do not have a presence in the market, some of your partners and allies are well-established. You can also recruit the leading partners in a segment.

IBM wants to be the global leader in health care information systems. There are tremendous opportunities to improve peoples' lives if providers and patients have a deeper knowledge with which to manage health, diagnose problems, and deliver cost-effective health care. Health care is an area of rapid change and tight budgets.

Soon, most providers and patients will want their information on wireless mobile devices. IBM partnered with PatientKeeper to run its record-management software on mobile devices.

IBM also works closely with Siemens Medical Solutions and McKesson so that IBM servers, storage, and Websphere software become platforms for comprehensive solutions implemented and managed by these leaders in healthcare information systems.

Market Research vs. Vision

All corporations need to make careful sales and marketing investment decisions. Strategy experts give us inconsistent advice about what drives strategy. Some tell us that our customers always drive strategy. Clayton Christensen, in *The Innovators Dilemma* shows how that approach can lead to disaster.

In the 1940s, IBM's initial market research showed the need for only seven computers in the

223

world! No one had even imagined personal computers. It was visionary scientists, not corporate marketing executives, who brought us into the age of information technology.

Customers offer excellent guidance to continuous improvement in their market. Continuous improvement is lead by customers, market segment leaders, and our strategic partners.

Customers usually offer poor guidance about disruptive technology in new markets. The best strategy may be to create a market that never existed. With disruptive technology, the best guides are often the visions of great entrepreneurs and innovators.

Summary

Customers provide the foundation for business growth. Customer relations improve when we invest in improved products and services to meet their needs. From a strong foundation of leadership with existing customers, there is an opportunity to expand within customer communities, with new products, and with new markets.

Protecting and expanding involves intelligent investment in marketing, hiring, product development, and service improvement. About 40% of this investment should be focused on existing customers. Another 40% should be focused on dominating specific market segments. 20% should be invested in creating and commercialize new products, or in expanding into new markets.

You have now looked at how great companies achieve market leadership, partner excellence, and sales leverage. Implement all of these in parallel, and you may create a Revenue Rocket.

Executive Action

➤ Invest 40% of your marketing, hiring, and product development in protecting and expanding business with existing customers.

➤ Invest 40% in dominating specific market segments where you can be the number one leader in revenue, profits and customer satisfaction.

➤ Creative leaders invest 20% in creating new "breakthrough" products, and in being first to market.

➤ Customer and cost leaders invest 20% in expanding into new markets.

Sales Action

➤ Be highly focused on the 20% of your customers that are most important.

➤ Allocate most sales time, and field marketing budget, to market segments where your firm has the highest share.

➤ Leverage strategic allies and channel partners who best meet the needs of key customers and markets.

15

Revenue Rocket

Implement strategy in this order:
1. **Market Leadership**
2. **Partner Excellence**
3. **Sales Leverage**

RECAPITULATION

One billion people are mesmerized watching their TVs as astronauts travel over 40,000 kilometers per hour, accelerating into space in defiance of earth's gravity. The launch infrastructure and team must be perfect. Precision aim is mandatory. 160 million horsepower is needed to lift the rocket off the ground.

People should equally admire a sales team that achieves record success, overcoming the overwhelming gravity of organizational inertia, and then accelerating through a meteor shower of competition. A foundation is developed with market leadership. Partner excellence creates a revenue "lift-off." Sales leverage takes success into the rarified stratosphere. Continued acceleration carries the most successful to new heights.

It is time to build a Revenue Rocket. You will soon launch your rocket to record sales. To reach the stars, a rocket needs direction and velocity. For you to reach the stars, you need strategy and execution. Aiming the rocket in the correct direction is critical.

Getting started is a lot like launching a rocket. If the rocket is a tenth of a degree off at launch, it can end up 1,000 miles off downrange.

—Craig Johnson
Chairman, Venture Law Group

Market Leadership

The best companies know better than to attack a major competitor on all fronts. Winners divide a large market into segments. They focus on a segment until they have number one share in that segment. Then they take their success to a related segment and lead there. They expand, segment by segment, until they are established in the broad market.

As they segment the market, more specific customer needs surface. They do better market research. They talk to industry leaders. They offer better services to meet specific market segment customer needs.

Revenue happens faster when you beat your competition to market with a better product or service. Revenue accelerates as you take business from competition. At first glance, sales executives are powerless to get products to market sooner. New products are the domain of engineers, technical specialists, and suppliers. In fact, sales executives should have key customers constantly engaged in product development. Successful sales people understand that part of their job is to get their customers involved in providing insight about needed services and product features.

One measure of leadership is in achieving better long-term customer relationships than your competition. For our customers, we are the best at cost, creativity, or customer intimacy. We build lifetime customer relationships based on one of these values. We accelerate our rocket with lightspeed response.

Partner Excellence

Mindshare is a key to accelerating channel revenue. New products are an opportunity to increase mindshare. Use new product announcements to build excitement with all sales channels. Train about the product, its applications, superior competitive positioning, sales, and support.

Give partners the tools to succeed such as brochures, marketing kits, proposal libraries, samples, demos and more. Make it easy to sell for partners to sell your products and services.

Disruptive products give you an opportunity to unseat your competition. Patience is required as you start with a leading customer in a leading market. Team with your strategic allies to create a complete, "bulletproof" solution to a problem that has been waiting for a solution. Slowly engage value partners as you expand to dominate one segment then the next.

Sales Leverage

To accelerate your revenue rocket into the stratosphere, you need to take your customers' experiences to the next level. Provide customers with the flexibility of using multiple channels for multiple needs. Provide customers with the convenience of multiple touchpoints. Encouraging everyone to work as a team with the ideal coverage model, compensation, communications, and relationship management.

Continued growth depends on using all sales channels effectively. To be a leader, you must have sales leverage. You must fine-tune the synergy between direct sales teams, channel partners, and eCommerce. Customer Intimate leaders invest in direct customer teams to sustain their competitive advantage. Creative leaders use direct teams to introduce innovative products, then emphasize channel partners appropriate to the stage of the product lifecycle. All leaders use eCommerce to give customers multiple touchpoints. Only Cost leaders use eCommerce to compete with channel partners.

Revenue Rocket

Revenue is accelerated with brand extension that creates additional sales for all partners. The Walt Disney Company is one of the world's most successful brands. Children and their families know that they will be entertained and delighted in Disney style, when they purchase a Disney product or service. Before a Disney movie is released, families watch television specials about how the movie is made. The specials are likely to be broadcast on The Walt Disney Company owned ABC channel, and the Disney cable channel.

People gladly pay to go to a theater and enjoy "The Little Mermaid." They love the music and purchase the CD. The young ones receive hours of entertainment from the added purchases of coloring books, storybooks, and tapes. Grandparents bring

Little Mermaid stuffed animals and dolls. Other relatives bring Little Mermaid games and toys. An aunt gives them the movie in video. An uncle buys the DVD version.

When the family reunion takes place, more likely than not, it is at a Disney theme park. On the way there, the selected radio station was Disney-owned.

Accelerate "Word-of-Mouth" Marketing

Customers within a large organization lead you to other customers within a large organization. AOL used this approach to dominate instant messaging. Users love the ability to see if their "buddies" are online, and exchange quick messages. Friends told friends where to signup, so that they could be added to their buddy list. If someone did not join, they were left out of gossip, gatherings, parties, job promotions, and so on. Join or risk social isolation. This "viral marketing" led to over 30 million people paying AOL over $20 per month for services that included instant messaging. Viral marketing is a modern variation of "word-of-mouth." The word spreads faster in this age of lightspeed response.

Word-of-mouth still has more power than the most expensive advertising campaigns. We are rewarded for going the extra mile for our customers. They tell others within their corporation. They will coach you on how to reach, and sell, those people. They will help if you have earned their respect and trust. Success spreads to other companies within a market segment.

From a position of established leadership, we can advance into new market segments. The process continues as we grow as a market leader.

Cisco

Cisco is the world's largest manufacturer of network switches. Most data traffic goes through their switches. Increasingly, your phone calls also go through their switches.

Employees consistently vote Cisco as one of the best companies to work for. Executives consistently vote Cisco near the top of Fortune's Most Admired Companies. At the dizzying heights of the stock market, Cisco's stock value exceeded General Electric, Microsoft, Exxon, and all other companies.

The path to success has been swift, but not easy. Cisco was founded in 1984 by the husband-and-wife team of Leonard Bosack and Sandra Lerner. They literally started their business in a Silicon Valley garage. Money was so tight, they had to take an added mortgage on the house, and convince friends to work for deferred pay. This type of small business is often referred to as "mom and pop." Due to the hardware and software engineering involved, Cisco did not sell its first network router until 1986.

From the beginning, Cisco has been a creative leader. Cisco asks customers about their needs in managing networks of growing complexity. Cisco innovates by creating continuous improvements, and by creating breakthrough solutions. Cisco builds lifetime customer relationships through sales, support, innovation, enterprise solutions, and industry solutions.

Market leadership started in segments, with Cisco first targeting universities, and then expanding into aerospace, government, and other industries. Cisco was first to market with a more intelligent network router. They carefully expanded in market segments until they attained market leadership.

Growing the business was not easy. Out of cash, the founders sold most of the business to venture capitalist Donald Valentine of Sequoia Capital. He brought in an experienced CEO, John Morgridge, to run the company. Five years after Cisco was started, they were only a $28 million company.

Cisco never lost its focus on creative leadership, lifetime customers and market leadership. Customers loved Cisco and their products. Cisco expanded its product line, so that organizations could scale the routers as network traffic increased. Cisco sold customers software to manage their networks. As Cisco's leadership grew, other hardware and software firms formed strategic alliances with Cisco. They ensured that their products worked with Cisco. Cisco became an industry platform.

Cisco is a sales channel leader. They correctly use direct sales to focus on strategic global accounts. Channel partners handle all other customers. Channel partners handle 80% of Cisco's 20 billion dollar business. eBusiness is not used to compete with sales and channels. Instead, eBusiness is used to make sales and channels more effective. Sales people do not touch orders. Almost all orders are handled electronically. Instead, salespeople focus on strategic customer issues.

Cisco has mindshare leadership with its channels. Channel partners receive extensive certification training from Cisco. E-learning, support, help libraries, sales tools, configuration tools, software updates and people are available to Cisco's partners 24 hours daily, seven days per week. Each sales person and technical person of each partner can create his or her own private Internet portal with Cisco. They get the tools and information of personal interest, presented the way they want it.

Cisco built a Revenue Rocket. Morgridge brought in John Chambers to build global sales and channels. In 1995, John Chambers was promoted to CEO of Cisco. John Chambers spends most of his time with customers. He listens, then expands the companies product and service offerings to meet their needs.

Cisco has steadily expanded with networking products millions of times faster than their early routers. Cisco expanded into high-speed optical switches. They expanded into wireless. They expanded into voice switching, video and storage. Cisco has strategically acquired 70 companies since 1993. This expansion protects and expands their position as the dominant platform for networking.

Being a leader does not guarantee that you grow in a straight line. The telecommunication industry meltdown of 2001 and 2002 forced Cisco to reduce its employees and write-off billions in inventory. It had aggressively expanded into telecommunications at a time when the industry experienced a major reversal. Smaller, nimble competitors, such as Ciena, Avici, Juniper and Sycamore brought disruptive technology to market. Former allies in wireless, storage and software became competitors.

Yet, Cisco continues to be the dominant leader in networking. It has taken advantage of the industry downturn to take market share from major rivals such as Lucent and Nortel. Cisco stays focused on creative leadership, market leadership, partner excellence, lifetime customer relationships, and sales leverage.

It is Time to Take Action

Congratulations for completing this book. You have reviewed strategies that create a roadmap for leadership and success. You have witnessed the battles of corporations vying to be first to market, then the market leader. You have learned about how they sustain their successes.

Executives are encouraged to review the most important executive actions that follow, and make them happen. Continue to listen to your customers. Customers share what must be done to sustain lifetime customer relationships.

Channel partners, sales and support people are encouraged to continue to speak on behalf of your customers. Sometimes it takes courage to be a customer advocate. Only the courageous succeed.

Executive Action

➤ With new products, be first to market.

➤ Expand from one market segment to related segments until you are the market share leader.

➤ First, introduce breakthrough products to a market segment with compelling need and low competitive barriers.

➤ Determine whether your company is a Cost, Customer, or Creative Leader.

➤ If you are a Cost Leader, invest more heavily in "inside sales people." Invest aggressively in eCommerce. Run a tight ship.

➤ If you are a Customer Intimate leader, invest more heavily in major account-customer teams lead by senior sales and service people.

➤ If you are a Creative Leader, invest heavily in introducing unique products and services faster than your competition. Run a loose ship.

➤ Identify the customers that generated 80% of last year's profits. Identify the customers that will generate 80% of next year's profits.

➤ Invest in providing improved products and services for the 20% of your customers who deliver 80% of the profits.

> ➤ Segment the market. Invest in dominating one segment at a time.

> ➤ Create a plan to turn your product family into the platform for thousands of products and services provided by other companies.

> ➤ Create a vice president of global channels and alliances, who is a peer to your vice president of global direct accounts.

> ➤ Create a channel coverage model matrix, with one dimension representing products and services and a second dimension representation market segments.

> ➤ Develop and use a comprehensive partner database that includes the partners' value-discipline (remember the 4 Cs again) and authorized products.

> ➤ Write a channel business plan including forecasts, goals, strategies, and tactics.

> ➤ Identify the target number of partners needed in each product category. Recruit and terminate partners to match the targets.

> ➤ Protect needed partner profit margins.

> ➤ Create marketing campaigns by product and market segment, which can be implemented by your partners with their money.

> ➤ Implement PRM.

➢ Run quarterly Channel Advisory Council.

➢ Have someone accountable for the success of strategic alliances.

➢ Understand the total-solution needs of your top customers.

➢ Assemble a team of channel partners and strategic alliances to meet those needs.

➢ Plan a co-marketing, brand building campaign with alliance partners in a market segment where your risks are minimal if the alliance collapses.

➢ Have an internally published innovation game plan.

➢ Have an externally published statement of direction.

➢ Use disruptive product offerings to leapfrog the competition and create new markets. Only involve channel partners that offer significant value in the targeted market segment.

➢ Use sustaining innovation to take competitive shares, reinforce your brand, and improve existing channel revenue.

➢ Invest 80% of your resources on the 20% of your channels most committed to your products and services.

- ➢ Assign strategic global accounts, not general territories, to direct sales teams.

- ➢ Meet with your top 10 channel partners and strategic allies. Commit to specific co-marketing and co-sales decisions.

- ➢ Make everyone customer-centric and partner-centric through executive leadership and training.

- ➢ Integrate corporate and channel marketing.

- ➢ Achieve quarterly financial goals through a process of promotions and channel-neutral discounts to final customers. Do not stuff the channels.

- ➢ Implement Partner Relationship Management (PRM) to automate marketing content management, sales leads, sales tracking, and MDF management

- ➢ If you already have PRM, integrate it with your backend databases and enterprise applications.

- ➢ Establish a customer advisory council.

- ➢ For top customers, ask your sales team for a plan to make the customer a partner.

- ➢ For customers strategic to your future, arrange for executive meetings.

> ➢ For customers that do not fit your leadership model, or who are marginally profitable, lower sales coverage, lower sales cost, and shrink their discounts.

> ➢ For customers that do not fit your core competencies, or who are unprofitable, end the relationship.

> ➢ Protect channel partners by displaying prices and discounts only to customers with private log-ins and passwords.

> ➢ Improve eCommerce by allowing customers to electronically order through their purchasing systems or private websites.

> ➢ Integrate your demand-chain with your enterprise applications and databases.

> ➢ Improve customer service by facilitating collaboration between your team, your customers, and collaboration between customers.

> ➢ Provide customers with the flexibility of using multiple channels for multiple needs.

> ➢ Provide customers with the convenience of multiple touchpoints.

> ➢ Plan to have inside and outside sales working together, using common systems and a common database.

➢ For major accounts, ensure that your sales team is compensation neutral regardless of whether an order is placed directly or through a channel partner.

➢ Expect surprise. Implement radar and encourage rapid response.

➢ Make integration of systems across the supply and demand chains a top priority with key customers and suppliers.

➢ Increase sales time. Do not have salespeople touch orders.

➢ Think global; act mobile.

➢ Invest 40% of your marketing, hiring, and product development in protecting and expanding business with existing customers.

➢ Invest 40% of the above in dominating specific market segments where you can be the number one leader in revenue, profits and customer satisfaction.

➢ Creative leaders invest 20% in creating new "breakthrough" products, and in being the first to market.

➢ Customer and cost leaders invest 20% in expanding into new markets.

Sales Action

➢ Understand the total-solution needs of your top customers.

➢ If your product is disruptive, focus on a few customers with compelling needs. Only involve channel partners who integrate solutions.

➢ If your competitor is first to market, protect your customers and partners by offering a range of services not available from the innovator.

➢ In customer meetings, focus on the areas where your company is the leader.

➢ If you sell for a Creative Leader, work with channel partners who are Customer Intimate and Creative leaders until the product sells in high volume.

➢ If you sell for a Cost Leader, use eCommerce and volume distribution to free your sales time.

➢ If you sell for a Customer Intimate Leader, get deeply involved with a few customers.

➢ Select one customer community which has been highly profitable for your firm and for which your firm offers core advantages.

➢ For your top market segment, join an industry association in that segment. Volunteer to join a committee or their board.

➢ Develop a portfolio of channel partners who cover your targeted market segments.

➢ Use disruptive product announcements to attack competition and change customer criteria for making decisions. For each customer, identify the channel partner that can best help expand your business.

➢ In your personal contact database, add a field for each partner that identifies whether their value-leadership (cost, creative, customer intimate, or confused).

➢ Have customer planning sessions with channel partners.

➢ Write profiles of the type of partners you now need to drive your channel recruiting.

➢ Plan a customer event and co-marketing campaign with channel partners, which focus on your top market segment.

➢ Train the best; terminate the rest.

➢ Be proactive in identifying and managing conflict (it is part of the job). Listen to all, summarize the issues, and recommend win-win solutions.

- ➢ Continually improve channel management by fine-tuning how everyone makes money.

- ➢ Assemble a team of channel partners and strategic alliances to meet the solution needs of each customer.

- ➢ Jump-start an alliance by bringing the partner into one opportunity.

- ➢ Build trust carefully. Start by sharing information and sales strategy about a customer where your risks are minimal if you lose the customer.

- ➢ Plan to co-market a program and customer event with your partners and alliances.

- ➢ Ensure that your top channel partners are fully prepared to answer questions and take orders on the day of a new product announcement.

- ➢ Use product launches as an opportunity to develop mindshare with your customers and channel partners.

- ➢ For disruptive products, start with the customer intimate leaders in one target segment.

- ➢ Sell services that ensure that your customers are always benefiting from the latest products and getting 24/7 support.

➢ Invest 80% of your resources in the 20% of your channels most committed to your products and services.

➢ Always encourage partners to have more sales and technical people who are knowledgeable about your products and services. Keep a database of trained partner people.

➢ Meet with your top 10 channel partners. Plan different marketing campaigns with each, using MDF.

➢ Partners and customers should be sold training and support programs that empower them to resolve their own problems 24/7.

➢ Clone success.

➢ Start each quarter with a specific plan and forecast to achieve 300% of quarter. Do not show the plan to management, or they will increase your goal. Execute the plan and you will never need to stuff the channels.

➢ Involve top partner-marketing executives in the design of new marketing campaigns.

➢ Completely learn your company's CRM and PRM. Use these systems to distribute leads, implement marketing, and track results.

➢ Implement a 5^3-lightspeed plan.

➢ Read customer annual reports, executive speeches, articles, and news for strategic customer directions and vision.

➢ Build a close-working sales team, with regular informal fun activities. Celebrate small success and the major success will follow.

➢ Plan a meeting with your top customer's executives and your executives to explore a partnership or joint venture.

➢ Free your valuable sales time. Train your customers to place all orders electronically.

➢ For your top 5 customers, sell your company and your customers on having a private website and extranet for each customer.

➢ Use the Internet for lightspeed response with lifetime customers.

➢ Invite your best partners to planning sessions with your major-account, direct-sales teams.

➢ Encourage partners to invite major-account, direct sales teams to fun off-site activities. Build teams.

➢ Ensure that there is publicity and credit to all the people when direct sales and partners work together and achieve customer success.

➢ When making sales calls, assume that your top customers know as much about your company, products, and services as you.

➢ Use your firm's CRM and PRM systems to get inside teams and partners and to handle routine actions. Focus on long-term opportunities and your plan to be 300% of goal.

➢ Empower customers to place online orders with your partners and with your inside salespeople. Do not touch another order.

➢ Leverage your valuable sales time with a palm computer/cell phone that integrates with your CRM and PRM.

➢ Be highly focused on the 20% of your customers that are most important.

➢ Allocate most sales time and field marketing budget to market segments where your firm has the highest share.

➢ Leverage strategic allies and channel partners who best meet the needs of key customers and markets.

Glossary

24/7 is shorthand for 24 hours per day, 7 days per week. Customers increasingly want to place orders and get service 24/7.

Account Executives (AEs) are the salespeople responsible for building lifetime customer relationships. For a given customer, an account executive must simultaneously build quarterly revenue and ensure customer delight in a relationship that is profitable for their corporation and the customer. The role of the AE is strategic, not transactional.

Channels of distribution are the components of the network of companies who resell your products and services. Large companies often have complex channels of distribution, including distributors between the company and specialized resellers.

Channel partners are the specific companies who take your products and services to market. They include retailers, resellers, wholesalers, strategic allies, and others.

Customer communities are groups of potential customers with similar characteristics. Customer communities are often divided by geography, type of business, need, demographics, and psychographics. A customer community is also a market segment.

Cost leaders drive efficiency and drive down sales cost. Cost leaders do the best job of saving their customers money with lower-cost products and by doing work for their customers. Cost leaders tend to be very-efficient, multi- billion-dollar firms. They achieve economies of scale.

Creative leaders develop breakthrough products and services. They often have a free-spirited corporate culture that encourages innovation.

Customer intimate leaders are in the people business. They are excellent at being responsive to the unique needs of each customer. The motto of a customer intimate leader is: "The customer is always right."

Customer Relationship Management (CRM) is the name for the strategies, processes, and software applications that enable people to work as a team in sales and support of customers.

Data warehouses extract information from the database used for transactions such as order entry and accounting. A data warehouse also includes information that helps with salespeople, customer support, and customer websites. A data warehouse organizes the information so that people can quickly find what is needed and use it effectively. A data warehouse helps organize marketing campaigns.

Direct sales usually involve a team from your corporation of account managers, inside sales people, and customer support, who work directly with your customers. They work closely with your top global accounts, and provide a direct link to your corporation.

Disruptive technology is breakthrough innovation that threatens a market's status quo. If the disruptive technology is widely adapted, the market leader is usually replaced; the value-chain from supplier to final customer is fundamentally changed.

eCRM connects people with integrated phone, email, messaging, and web browser to customer history, CRM sales and support applications.

Enterprise Resource Planning (ERP) describes the software and processes that large organizations use to run their businesses. Applications include accounting, order processing, production planning, human resources and more.

Inside salespeople live on the telephone. These jobs are often based in sophisticated call centers, where they can work as teams, handling calls from customers and to customers.

Legacy systems are older information systems, often running on mainframe and mini-computers. It takes some effort to integrate them with a corporation's PCs, wireless devices, and eBusiness.

Lightspeed response involves responding to your customer faster and better than all your competitors. Customers want to reach your people immediately. They want their computer systems linked to yours for automatic information and response. Customers want to work at the speed of light.

Lightspeed 5^3: Select your 5 most important customers. Select the 5 most important decision makers and influencers for each of those customers. Give each person 5 ways to reach you for lightspeed response such as your cell phone, your home phone, your alphanumeric pager, your instant message ID, and your email.

Markets consist of all the customers and potential customers for a product or service.

Marketing is communicating with the market in ways that encourage customers to increase their business with you.

Market segment is part of a larger market. A market segment is a group of potential customers with similar characteristics. **See customer communities.**

Marketing Development Funds (MDF) encourage channel partners to market specific products; some manufacturers create MDF accounts for each channel partner. Partners are reimbursed from these MDF accounts when they spend money implementing specific marketing campaigns. For example, 2% of all partner sales may accrue in an MDF account. When partners conduct preapproved advertising, they are reimbursed from their MDF accounts.

Mindshare is the amount of time that your channel partners think about your products and services. You want your partners' minds and hearts. Mindshare leads to partner loyalty.

Original Equipment Manufacturers (OEMs) create a complete product that includes another supplier's technology or product. Hewlett-Packard is an OEM for "Intel Inside".

Partner Relationship Management (PRM) allows you to know about your channel partners and their customers. PRM is made up of the strategies, processes and software applications that allow companies to work closely with their channel partners. PRM allows you to automatically distribute information, prices, and more to your channels. PRM gives you realtime information about what your channels are marketing, learning, proposing and selling.

Resellers sell products for a variety of firms. Resellers compete on price and customer convenience. In different industries, they go by names such as retailers, eCommerce sites, rep firms, and distributors. For example, Wal-Mart is an important reselling partner of Coca-Cola.

Solution providers make products part of complete customer solutions. In different industries, they go by various names, such as system integrators, service providers, original equipment manufacturers (OEMs), and value-added resellers.

Strategic alliances typically involve the cooperation of two corporations in their sales and marketing. They normally do not resell each other's products. Instead they work together to meet common goals. Alliances can involve several firms. Most alliances become temporary "marriages of convenience" which fail.

Strategic partners complement products and make them more important to customers. They often do not resell the products. Oracle software makes Sun Microsystems computers more valuable to many customers, and vice-versa. They are strategic partners.

Stuff the channels is an expression that refers to convincing distributors and resellers to take large inventory positions.

Two-tiered distribution. Large companies often have complex channels of distribution including distributors between the company and specialized resellers.

Acknowledgements

Thank you to all the channel partners and salespeople with whom I have worked. You speak passionately on behalf of your customers. You are their advocates. You take the exciting products of your suppliers, combine them with your custom services, and deliver complete solutions to your customers. Hopefully, I have captured some of your invaluable lessons in this book.

Geoffrey Moore has a gift for bringing clarity to business strategy. His models for the technology-adoption life cycle are at the heart of corporate marketing strategy. Now, executives are actively implementing his recommendations about developing lasting competitive advantages by developing core and shedding context. I greatly appreciate the times that Dr. Moore has helped, sharing insights, and kind words.

Guy Kawasaki is inspirational. He brings people together for noble causes, creating a legion of evangelists. I thank him for his wonderful speeches, wise and witty books, and kind words.

I'd like to extend my thanks to those interviewed, especially Joe Womack, for insights about the state of channels and the future of sales. Thank you to those who responded to the research survey.

The sharing of information on the Internet is invaluable when authoring a business strategy book such as *Revenue Rocket*. In sessions that were once behind closed doors, I was able to hear executives present their strategies and quarterly results, then answer the tough questions in streaming-video analyst conferences. Corporate presentations, papers, SEC filings, and partner websites were available. Deeper insights came from a variety of print and online publications including *The Wall Street Journal, Hoovers.com, VARBusiness, Selling Power, Fortune, Business Week, Business 2.0, and Red Herring.* Thanks to Google.com for putting the world at our fingertips.

I greatly appreciate the busy frontline channel managers and senior executives who read early drafts of this book and then contributed. What you are reading is far different in structure, flow, and content from the first version. Thank you to Bob Eubank for recommending that each chapter have a big idea and action items. He reminded me that the book must have value, even for an executive reading it on a short flight. Careful readings, and specific improvements, came from Kackie Cohen, Vipin Kumar, Emil Chiang, Harrison Chan, and Philippe Lavie. Philippe's expertise in PRM was most helpful. Athol Foden, Joanne Hasegawa, and Amy Fritz were especially helpful in their ideas about positioning and marketing the book.

For ten years, the strategies and action items in this book have been presented, tested, challenged, and refined in hundreds of workshops and in consulting with sales, marketing, and channel managers. Thank you to all who helped refine these models.

From the very beginning, my brother Keith Short has helped me shape this book. Long hikes, insightful dialogues, and lots of encouragement got me through the rough spots. Ron Lindsay, a valued friend and successful channel executive, created the title "Revenue Rocket." The love I share with Marci has brightened my life. Thank you for all your love and support.

Jeff Schachner, a close friend and outstanding sales-account executive, introduced me to Peter Griffes, President of ProStar Publications. It has been exciting to work with the ProStar team, which includes Peter, Ron Ligrano, Diana Hunter, Melody Nicholson, Michael Jaffe, and Gil Hackel.

The channel partners who create better customer solutions each day shaped the best lessons in this book. I appreciate all the knowledge, which they have shared. I would value your insights as well. Feel free to send me a note at john@optimarkworks.com.

With many thanks and best wishes,

John Addison

www.optimarkworks.com